It's Simply Time

TO BE A LIGHT IN THE DARKNESS

Kimberly Hooper

WESTBOW
PRESS®
A DIVISION OF THOMAS NELSON
& ZONDERVAN

WestBow Press books may be ordered through booksellers or by contacting:

WestBow Press
A Division of Thomas Nelson & Zondervan
1663 Liberty Drive
Bloomington, IN 47403
www.westbowpress.com
844-714-3454

Scriptures are taken from the NEW AMERICAN STANDARD BIBLE®, Copyright © 1960, 1962,
1963, 1968, 1971, 1972, 1973, 1975, 1977, 1995 by The Lockman Foundation. Used by permission.

ISBN: 979-8-3850-2071-3 (sc)
ISBN: 979-8-3850-2072-0 (e)

Library of Congress Control Number: 2024904579

Print information available on the last page.

WestBow Press rev. date: 07/10/2024

ACKNOWLEDGMENTS

I am incredibly grateful to my Lord and Savior Jesus Christ, who has completely transformed my life through the amazing gifts of the cross and His redeeming love. It is through His sacrifice that I have found true redemption and purpose.

I also want to express my deep gratitude to those who have played a significant role in my spiritual journey many years ago. First, I am thankful to Jan Silkman for giving me my first Bible and teaching me how to connect with God through prayer. Jan, you have been instrumental in shaping my faith, and I am forever grateful.

Linda Knott, you have been a guiding light in my life, showing me the importance of studying God's word and seeking answers to my questions. Your teaching has equipped me to dive deeper into biblical truths and grow in my understanding of God's word.

Trish Folker, I am indebted to you for imparting the significance of our American Christian Heritage. Through your guidance, I have come to appreciate how God's hand of providence has shaped our nation, and how the principles of self-government align with biblical values. Thank you for helping open my eyes to these truths.

I cannot forget to thank Karen Faith, my dear sister in Yeshua, who has always encouraged me to embrace the call of Esther in these times. As a Jew and Gentile, we have witnessed the miraculous when we stand united. You truly are my way cool angel friend.

A special thank you goes to Sharon Marosi, my dear friend, for her selfless support in this project. Your dedication to Jesus and His kingdom is truly admirable.

Lastly, I want to take a moment to express my heartfelt gratitude to my husband, Sam. You may not always be in the spotlight, but your quiet support and encouragement have meant the world to me.

And now, to my beautiful children, Melissa and Grant. You are the greatest blessing in my life, and being your Mama brings me endless joy. I love you both more than words can express.

Also a special shout-out to my adorable grandson, Hudson. You are the apple of my eye and the light of our family. Kiki loves you so much.

Thank you all for being a part of my journey and for filling my life with love and meaning.

A WORD FROM THE AUTHOR

When I look back on my early days as a new believer, I can't help but feel immense gratitude for the godly women who took me under their wings. They selflessly invested their time and effort discipling me in the Word of God and showing me what it truly means to be a follower of Jesus Christ. Through their guidance, I learned the importance of studying the Bible in context, praying the Scriptures, and applying biblical principles to my life. They taught me how to navigate the highs and lows of life as a believer, and they exemplified what it means to walk with Jesus.

But as I engage in conversations today, I can't help but notice a concerning decline in the depth of people's understanding and ability to articulate their Christian faith. It breaks my heart to witness this lack of knowledge and confidence in proclaiming the truth of God's word. Even more disheartening is the fear that seems to grip many individuals, preventing them from standing up for biblical truth. The fear of rejection, criticism, and even alienation from their own family members, work colleagues, and sometimes fellow church members holds them back from boldly representing Christ.

My friend, within these pages, I implore you to reflect on the urgent call to be salt and light in this world. It is a call to unashamedly proclaim the truth of God's word and live out our faith without compromise. Now is the time for us to rise up, equipped with a deep understanding of Scripture and boldness that can only come from knowing who we are in Christ. Let us not be discouraged by challenges but rather be encouraged by the God who goes before us. As I share my journey and the wisdom learned over many years, I invite you to invest time in studying the Word of God, praying fervently, and surrounding yourself with a community of believers. Together, we will find the courage to stand firm in biblical truth, even in the face of opposition, and speak life in a world that so desperately needs it. Let us press on, always mindful of the role we play in advancing God's kingdom and bringing glory to His Name.

May we never forget the blessing of those who poured into us. May we in turn be a blessing as we disciple others to live out their faith confidently and passionately. Together, let us be a generation that seeks after God, studies His word, and fearlessly proclaims His truth. The time is now.

The things that you have heard from me in the presence of many witnesses, entrust these to faithful men who will be able to teach others also.
(II Timothy 2:2)

May God richly bless you as begin this study. May the Lord shine His Light upon you and protect you as you bring His Truth to a world that desperately needs Jesus.

Welcome to the Journey.

Kimberly Hooper

CONTENTS

God's Plumb Line 1

Cultivating a Biblical Worldview 11

The Promised Helper 19

Living the Surrendered Life 27

The Path to Success 39

Abiding in the True Vine 45

Blueprints of Grace 59

God is Sovereign 67

From Doubt to Confidence 75

Perseverance, Faith, and the Birth of a Nation 81

The Church in Society 91

Running the Race 103

GOD'S PLUMB LINE

Discerning Truth from Error

What Is a Plumb Line?

A plumb line is a weight suspended from a string and used as a vertical reference line. When used in carpentry, for instance, a plumb line ensures that everything is aligned, justified, and centered.

What Is God's Plumb Line?

The Bible is the account of God's infinite love and redemption for humankind. God created humankind in His image with the ability to choose good or evil. He established the way for us to know Him and to have a relationship with Him through His plan of redemption. The Bible shows us the way to walk uprightly before a holy God, aligned, justified, and centered on **truth**, as God intended.

For those who put their faith in God, the plumb line is the **Bible**. It is our reference point for living in a right relationship with the God of all Creation. The Bible establishes our worldview, based on truth.

How Can We Know That We Are Living the Way God Intended?

We compare our thoughts, emotions, and actions to God's plumb line. When we do not live as God intended, the Bible calls this sin. In Hebrew, sin is defined as *"chata,"* which means to miss the mark or to incur guilt in morality or righteousness.

> Therefore, to one who knows the right thing to do and does not do it, to him it is sin. (James 4:17)

When we observe our society exchanging what is good for what is evil, we see that God's plumb line has been disregarded. The Bible tells us that there will come a time when "good will be called evil and evil will be called good." I think we can all agree that we are living in that time.

A plumb line is not a moving target. It is not based on individual opinions or preferences. It hangs true no matter what.

ALIGNING YOURSELF TO THE PLUMB LINE OF GOD IS THE FIRST STEP IN LIVING YOUR LIFE THE WAY GOD INTENDED.

What Does God's Word Say About His plumb line?

> And I will make justice the measuring line, and righteousness the plumb line. (Isaiah 28:17)

> This is what He showed me: The Lord was standing by a vertical wall with a plumb line in His hand. And the Lord said to me, "What do you see, Amos?" And I said, "A plumb line," Then the Lord said, "Behold, I am about to put a plumb line in the midst of My people Israel; I will spare them no longer." (Amos 7:7–8)

When God said He was setting a plumb line among His people, He was declaring an end to their attempts to justify their crooked ways. The Word of God was to be their standard. God does not negotiate His laws nor change them to suit cultural whims. God's moral law is the plumb line against which we determine right and wrong.

> Sanctify them in the truth; Your word is truth. (John 17:17)

We are called to align our lives according to God's plumb line rather than trying to align His plumb line to our agendas or worldviews. I have heard women say, "God understands my heart," almost as a justification for the sin they are living in.

The truth is, God knows your heart and He loves you, but He will never compromise His word. It is up to us to study God's word, discern His heart, and do the best we can to align our lives to His standards and not to sin against Him. For us to make godly decisions we first have to be connected to the one who will give us the mind of Christ.

Read Proverbs 16:9 and 20:24

According to these verses, what is your role as you seek to align your life with God's plumb line?

How can you apply the concept of God being the ultimate director in your decision making processes, based on these scriptures?

The Problem

We are separated from God by our sins and cannot know and experience God's plan for our lives apart from atonement for our sins. We have been born into sin and deserve to be punished for that sin. The Bible clearly states, "For the wages of sin is death, but the free gift of God is eternal life in Christ Jesus our Lord." (Romans 6:23)

> For all have sinned and fall short of the glory of God. (Romans 3:23)

Sin leads us to a state of brokenness, a truth that we witness in our society. As the Bible tells us, "For they exchanged the truth of God for a lie, and worshiped and served the creature rather than the Creator, who is blessed forever." (Romans 1:25)

It is in this brokenness that we come to understand our need for something greater.

The Solution

> For God so loved the world, that He gave His only Son, so that everyone who believes in Him will not perish, but have eternal life. (John 3:16)

In a powerful moment recorded in Acts 16:30–31, the Philippian jailer asked Paul and Silas, "Sirs, what must I do to be saved?" Paul and Silas responded, "Believe in the Lord Jesus, and you will be saved, you and your household."

Jesus Christ is the ultimate answer to sin. God made it possible for every one of us to have a personal connection with Him through His Son, Jesus Christ. He came down to earth and lived in perfect accordance with God's plan. He willingly sacrificed His life, shedding His blood, to pay the price for all our sins. This act forever bridged the gap between humanity and God. Jesus rescued us by giving us what we could never attain on our own.

When we accept Jesus Christ as our Lord and Savior, we are telling God that we accept His incredible gift of love and salvation, which allows us to have a restored relationship with Him.

> But (He) emptied Himself, taking the form of a bondservant, being made in the likeness of men. Being found in appearance as a man, He humbled Himself by becoming obedient to the point of death, even death on a cross! (Philippians 2:7–8)

> Having canceled the certificate of debt consisting of decrees against us, which was hostile to us; and He has taken it out of the way, having nailed it to the cross. (Colossians 2:14)

What Is Your Response?

Only when we admit our sin and brokenness, ask for forgiveness, and individually receive Jesus Christ as our Lord and Savior can we know and experience God's love and plan for our lives.

The time is fulfilled, and the kingdom of God is at hand; repent and believe in the gospel. (Mark 1:15)

For by grace you have been saved through faith, and this is not of yourselves, it is the gift of God; not a result of works, so that no one may boast. (Ephesians 2:8–9)

If we profess Jesus as our Lord, His life, ministry, and teaching become our plumb line. As recipients of this wonderful gift of faith, we are called to start living according to the instructions for life and godliness found in the Bible.

That if you confess with your mouth Jesus as Lord, and believe in your heart that God raised Him from the dead, you will be saved. (Romans 10:9)

For it is God who is at work in you, both to desire and to work for His good pleasure. (Philippians 2:13)

Salvation is the gift of God, but like any gift, it only has value if we take it and claim it as our own.

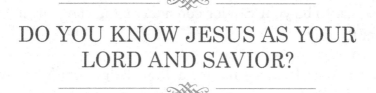

DO YOU KNOW JESUS AS YOUR LORD AND SAVIOR?

The good news is that it is never too late to turn to God and accept His gift of salvation. He is always ready and willing to receive us with open arms, no matter how far we may have drifted or how long we may have rejected Him. If you have never accepted God's gift of salvation, you can do that today. By choosing to trust in Jesus Christ alone for your sins you can experience the transformative power of His love and be assured of everlasting life.

When you put your trust and faith in Jesus, the Bible says, "You will not perish but have everlasting life." (John 3:16).

All you have to do is accept this beautiful gift, open it, and believe in everything that God desires to grant you as His cherished daughter.

Read Hebrews 3:12–19

What are the dangers of having an unbelieving heart when it comes to the things of God?

We need to encourage one another daily, to guard against unbelief and continued disobedience, and hold firmly to faith to avoid falling into the same pattern of unbelief and rebellion.

Read John 14:6

What claims does Jesus make about Himself in this passage? How do you understand those claims personally?

Personally understanding these claims means that you recognize that Jesus is the ultimate source of guidance, truth, and eternal life. If you are ready to put your trust in Jesus to be your Savior consider using the prayer below to make this commitment today.

> Heavenly Father, I am a sinner. I acknowledge that You gave Your only Son, Jesus, to die for my sins. I confess that I am a sinner. Thank You for sending Jesus to die for me and for calling me as Your daughter. I do not want to live any longer after the world's standards, but I desire to be separate from the world, to learn Your ways, and to grow in faith. I give You my life and surrender my will to You so that I may learn how to walk in a way that pleases You. Teach me in the days ahead how to follow Your will for my life. Teach me to obey Your commandments. Thank You for giving me Your Holy Spirit, who will teach me how to understand the Bible and apply Your teachings to my life.
>
> In Jesus's name, amen.

If you have prayed this prayer, welcome to the family of God. Jesus loves you so much and He is excited to have a personal relationship with you. Just think, you are now walking hand in hand with Jesus as He guides you on this beautiful journey ahead.

As you study God's word that you will learn how to build a personal foundation of morality, integrity, and ethical behavior. You will gain wisdom to apply spiritual discernment in your life choices and align your life according to His principles.

Putting your trust in Jesus marks the beginning of living a set-apart life unto God. He will guide you every step of the way, leading you toward a life filled with purpose, joy, and fulfillment. Get ready to experience the incredible blessings that come with being part of God's family.

THE BIBLE BECOMES YOUR PLUMB LINE FOR LIFE.

Applying what the Bible teaches is the duty of all Christians. Paul in the book of Philippians says, "Whatever you have learned or received or heard from me, or seen in me, put into practice. And the God of peace will be with you." (Philippians 4:9).

When we apply biblical truth to our lives, God Himself promises to be with us.

> The psalmist said, "Your word I have treasured in my heart, that I might not sin against You." (Psalm 119:11)

As you seek to know God more, plan regular times to *come away* and spend intentional and focused time with Him. This devoted time of communion with God will not only nourish your spirit but will also help you stay on track and steer you away from sin.

- How do you think regular and intentional time spent with God will help you to stay on track and avoid sin?

- What are some practical ways that you can apply biblical truth in your everyday life?

MAKE A FRESH COMMITMENT TODAY TO SIT AT THE FEET OF JESUS.

The wisdom found in the Bible is essential for deepening one's faith and spiritual strength, you cannot grow strong without it.

> I have treasured the words of His mouth more than my daily bread. (Job 23:12)

As the Word of God takes root, it becomes the necessary guide for navigating life's challenges and forming a strong spiritual foundation. By committing to **READ**, **STUDY**, **REFLECT**, and **APPLY** God's word, you will grow in your faith and understanding. Through this practice you will develop a deeper connection with God and gain valuable insights for living a fulfilling and purposeful life.

READ Just as we need daily food to survive, we need the spiritual food that God has provided in His word. Reading the Bible is not just an activity, but an essential habit for our spiritual growth and understanding. It is through reading the Bible that we gain insight into God's character, find guidance for our lives, and draw closer to Him. Just like physical food nourishes our bodies, the words in the Bible nourish our souls. We cannot grow spiritually strong without it.

> Blessed is the one whose delight is in the law of the Lord, and in His law he meditates day and night. (Psalm 1:1–2)

My Commitment: I will read God's word daily to align my beliefs to God's plumb line.

STUDY As you study, you will discover who God is, examples of His faithfulness through the ages, and so much more. As you learn the stories and examples taught in the Bible, you will be able to discern the ways of God. The Bible is not just another book, but a treasure of wisdom and guidance that will empower you to walk by faith, to find hope in challenging times, to find comfort in times of sorrow, and to find direction for your life.

> If you seek her as silver and search for her as for hidden treasures; then you will discern the fear of the Lord and discover the knowledge of God. (Proverbs 2:3–4)

My Commitment: I will be diligent to present myself approved to God as a workman who will not be ashamed, accurately handling the word of truth. (2 Timothy 2:15)

REFLECT Take time to reflect on what you are learning. Meditate on the wisdom found in God's word and soak in its deep significance. As you read, think about how it applies to your life and note areas where you need to adjust the way you think and behave. This reflective practice not only helps you grow in your understanding of Scripture, but also deepens your relationships with Jesus. Remember to take time to pause, reflect, and allow God's word to shape your heart and mind.

My Commitment: I will read the Bible to gain new insights each time I study. I will think about what I am learning, and I will make the necessary adjustments in my life. I will let the plumb line of God's word convict me regarding the changes I need to make in my thoughts, beliefs, and actions.

APPLY As Christians, it is important for us to not only read and know the Word of God but also to apply it to our lives. Simply acquiring knowledge is not enough; we are called to put what we learn into action. This preparation equips us to live out our beliefs and be a positive witness for Christ. It's not enough to just hear the word, we must be and do what it says.

> We are not to be conformed to this world, but rather to be transformed by the renewing of our mind, able to test and discern what the will of God is, that good and acceptable will of God. (Romans 12:2)

> But prove yourselves doers of the word, and not just hearers who deceive themselves. (James 1:22)

My Commitment: I will seek to be intentional in applying the Word of God to my life so that I may live in obedience and faithfulness to my Heavenly Father. I seek to be ready to articulate my faith and share it with others. I desire for people to see the love and truth of Jesus in my life.

Walk It Out

1. How can reading the Bible help you to align your beliefs with God and understanding the plumb line?

_____

_____

_____

_____

_____

2. What are the benefits of studying the Bible and building a solid foundation for understanding and applying God's truth?

_____

_____

_____

_____

_____

3. Of the four areas read, study, reflect, and apply, which one do you need to work on? Write Your Own Personal Commitment about the area that you chose:

_____

_____

_____

_____

_____

CULTIVATING A BIBLICAL WORLDVIEW

LESSON 2

Discovering the Path of Truth

How Do I Discover God's Viewpoint?

God's viewpoint is made clear through His word, the Bible. Aligning our ideas and beliefs to God's viewpoint results in a *biblical worldview*. It begins with the Creator of all things.

> God created man in His own image, in the image of God He created him; male and female He created them. God blessed them; and God said to them, "Be fruitful and multiply, and fill the earth, and subdue it; and rule over the fish of the sea and over the birds of the sky and over every living thing that moves on the earth." (Genesis 1:27–28)

> Then the Lord God took the man and put him into the garden of Eden to cultivate it and keep it. (Genesis 2:15)

Read Genesis 3

What happened when Adam and Eve sinned and how did this impact the whole world?

Despite the curse of sin, God did not abandon humanity. He had a plan of redemption and made a way for our salvation from the very beginning.

> And I will put enmity between you and the woman, and between your seed and her seed; He shall bruise you on the head, and you shall bruise him on the heel. (Genesis 3:15)

The promise given in Genesis 3:15 was ultimately fulfilled through Jesus Christ. This lays the foundation for us to understand God's love, grace, and provision to restore man's relationship with Him.

> For the Son of Man has come to seek and to save that which was lost. (Luke 19:10)

Read Isaiah 65:17–25

What does God say about the former things when He comes again?

A biblical worldview centers on the belief that God's divine plan is revealed through the Bible. Those who embrace a biblical worldview align their lives with God's commands and make choices that are consistent with the instructions that are in God's word.

In a world that often promotes the wisdom of man over the wisdom of God, a biblical worldview challenges us to seek truth from the Scriptures, to test every belief and ideology against the word of God, and to align our lives with what is pleasing to Him. It reminds us that we are citizens of a heavenly kingdom, called to be salt and light in a world that desperately needs the transformative power of the gospel.

FOLLOW ME

Jesus perfectly modeled living according to the biblical worldview. When Jesus walked on the earth, He invited His disciples to walk with Him. He said to them, *"Follow Me."* Then Jesus called the crowd to Him, along with His disciples, and He said, "If anyone would come after me, he must deny himself and take up his cross and follow Me." (Mark 8:34)

When Jesus called His disciples, they dropped everything and followed Him. They couldn't possibly understand who He was, but there was something about Him that they could not resist. It would take time for the disciples to learn that Jesus was not just another teacher or holy man, but rather the long-awaited Messiah. He was the One sent into the world to save them—and us—from sin.

Jesus calls us to surrender our lives completely, and to *follow Him.*

> Do not suppose that I have come to bring peace to the earth. I did not come to bring peace, but a sword. For I have come to turn a man against his father, a daughter against her mother, a daughter-in-law against her mother-in-law, a man's enemies will be the members of his own household. Anyone who loves their father or mother more than Me is not worthy of Me; anyone who loves their son or daughter more than Me is not worthy of Me; and anyone who does not take up their cross and follow Me is not worthy of Me. Whoever finds their life will lose it, and whoever loses their life for my sake will find it. (Matthew 10:34–39)

COUNT THE COST

Jesus never softened the truth about what it meant to follow Him. He made it clear that His followers might be persecuted for the sake of righteousness. Jesus said that people will hate His followers because of their commitment to Him. The truth is, to follow Jesus requires you to make difficult choices regarding your priorities. To be a true disciple you must prioritize God's kingdom values over your love for and devotion to anyone or anything else. This does not mean that you disregard others; rather, you make your love for God your first priority.

> You shall love the Lord your God with all your heart, and with all your soul, and with all your mind. This is the great and foremost commandment. (Matthew 22:37–38)

Our faith in Jesus must be extraordinarily strong so that we will not turn away when times of persecution inevitably come. It is undeniable that we are facing incredibly challenging times. Without question, we are in the last days. As believers, we must be wise as serpents and innocent as doves as we discern the difference between what is good and what is evil. Regardless of when Christ returns, each of us is responsible to God to learn and live by biblical principles, demonstrating the character of Jesus and making the truth of God known to others.

In our nation, the adversaries of God have gained considerable influence in our land and are posing a serious threat by attempting to strip away our fundamental rights as humans and suppress the voice of the Church. They employ methods such as cancel culture, political correctness, and various forms of intimidation to achieve their objective. We cannot passively observe while the foundations are being destroyed. Instead, we need to be fully prepared to boldly assert the truth found in the Scriptures to counter the deceptive falsehoods presented by those who are blinded by the enemy.

> If the foundations are destroyed, what can the righteous do? (Psalm 11:3)

> In whose case the god of this world has blinded the minds of the unbelieving so that they might not see the light of the gospel of the glory of Christ, who is the image of God. (2 Corinthians 4:4)

It is crucial for us to acquire an understanding of the Bibles teaching concerning Creation and God's original intentions for humanity, marriage, and societal structure. Are you aware that the Truth reproaches and corrects those who are in error? This statement may upset individuals who are not seeking the truth and we currently observe this opposition acting out in society today.

Jesus faced hatred because He fearlessly proclaimed the Truth. We should anticipate nothing less when confronting the adversary. God is in control of the battle and has called upon all believers to join Him in the fight to protect the foundations of truth and to turn people back to God.

> For behold, darkness will cover the earth and deep darkness the peoples; but the Lord will rise upon you and His glory will appear upon you. (Isaiah 60:2)

> But sanctify Christ as Lord in your hearts, always being ready to make a defense to everyone who asks you to give an account for the hope that is in you, yet with gentleness and reverence. (1 Peter 3:15)

> Those from among you will rebuild the ancient ruins; you will raise up the age-old foundations; and you will be called the repairer of the breach, the restorer of the streets in which to dwell. (Isaiah 58:12)

We need to wholeheartedly pray for a genuine revival and spiritual awakening, remaining steadfast in America's Christian roots as we promote the Christian faith with stronger conviction. **It's simply time** for the members of the Christian community to wholeheartedly proclaim God's Truth to our culture.

REDEEM WHAT IS BROKEN WHILE LIFTING WHAT IS SACRED.

Where Do We Begin?

We begin by applying God's word in our own lives with a commitment to live daily in the light of biblical truth. Only as we dispel the darkness in our thinking will we become a light to others.

How Can We Influence a Lost World?

Jesus hand-picked a diverse group of twelve disciples to accompany Him. Despite being ordinary men, they had a tremendous impact on the world.

How About You?

Jesus has also chosen you to serve a vital role within His Church. He has invited you to follow Him, to radiate the presence of God's kingdom in this world.

> Just as You sent Me into the world, I also send them into the world. (John 17:18)

> For we are His workmanship, created in Christ Jesus for good works, which God prepared beforehand so that we would walk in them. (Ephesians 2:10)

> You shall love the Lord your God with all your heart and with all your soul and with all your mind and with all your strength. (Mark 12:30)

> Teaching them to observe all that I have commanded you; and lo, I am with you always, even to the end of the age. (Matthew 28:20)

Read Isaiah 40:31

What encouragement is this to you at this time in history?

Read Galatians 2:20

Meditate on Paul's motivation for living. What perspective should we have as we live for Jesus?

Read Zechariah 8:16–17

What are believers commanded to do in this verse? What do you think will happen if the Church remains silent?

Write about a time when you followed God's call, and it was difficult to do:

- What did God call you to do, or what decision did you have to make?

- What was happening around you?

- Who else was with you?

- What emotions did you experience as you obeyed that call of God?

- What was the outcome?

Walk It Out

Read Jeremiah 32:27, 1 Peter 3:10–12, 1 Corinthians 3:6–7, and Psalm 127:1
Share your thoughts about each passage.

_____

_____

_____

Read Ephesians 4:15, 25, 29
What does it mean to speak the Truth in love?

_____

_____

_____

Read 2 Chronicles 7:14
Take some time to pray for America.

_____

_____

_____

Read Psalm 90:12 and Colossians 4:5
What are the consequences if we don't redeem the time and share the Truth with those who lack wisdom?

_____

_____

_____

THE PROMISED HELPER

Empowering our Journey

If a lamp is not plugged into a power source it will not be able to generate light. It is the same for us when we attempt to do what God is calling us to do, but we are not plugged into our Power Source—the Holy Spirit. When we try to succeed in our strength, we become frustrated, overwhelmed, and burned out. It is reassuring to know that God does not expect us to live in our own strength. He promised to send us a Helper.

John's Gospel recorded the words of Jesus regarding the Holy Spirit:

> But I tell you the truth, it is to your advantage that I go away; for if I do not go away, the Helper will not come to you; but if I go, I will send Him to you. And He, when He comes, will convict the world concerning sin and righteousness and judgment; concerning sin, because they do not believe in Me. (John 16:7–9)

> He will glorify Me, for He will take of Mine and will disclose it to you. All things that the Father has are Mine; therefore I said that He takes of Mine and will disclose it to you. (John 16:14–15)

What Does It Mean To Be Led By the Holy Spirit?

The role of the Holy Spirit in your life is to guide you into all truth, fill you with the desire for righteousness, and to help you live a life that is pleasing to God.

The Holy Spirit will convict you and steer you away from the things that can trip you up, things such as materialism, greed, pride, and lust.

Being plugged into the Power Source is evidenced in your life as love, joy, peace, patience, kindness, goodness, faithfulness, gentleness, and self-control—the fruit of the Spirit. As you yield to His leading, your words, lifestyle choices, and overall conduct will align with God's plumb line.

A believer's life should look different from the lives of those who follow the ways of the world. When people observe a believer, they should see the character of Jesus, the godly traits that set us apart as His disciples.

> For all who are being led by the Spirit of God, these are sons of God. (Romans 8:14)

> But I say, walk by the Spirit, and you will not carry out the desire of the flesh. (Galatians 5:16)

> Let no one look down on your youthfulness, but rather in speech, conduct, love, faith, and purity, show yourself an example of those who believe. (1 Timothy 4:12)

> The glory which You have given Me I have given to them, that they may be one, just as We are one; I in them and You in Me, that they may be perfected in unity, so that the world may know that You sent Me, and loved them, even as You have loved Me. (John 17:22–23)

> By this all people will know that you are My disciples: if you have love for one another." (John 13:35)

YOU HAVE A UNIQUE STORY.

The Great Commission, as defined by the Bible, is the commandment given by Jesus to His followers to spread the gospel message to all nations, making disciples, baptizing them, and teaching them to obey His teachings. It is about sharing the good news of salvation and inviting others to follow Jesus, ultimately leading them to a personal relationship with Him.

As a believer, the unique experiences, skills, and gifts that are part of your story serve as a witness of God's faithfulness in your life. As you share your testimony, talents, and God-given abilities with others, you demonstrate the transformative power that Jesus can have in the life of a believer.

Read Matthew 28:18–20

What are the key components of the Great Commission?

No matter what God calls you to do, He will equip you to fulfill that mission in the power of the Holy Spirit as you yield to His will. This is the same Holy Spirit who equipped Jesus to complete the mission that His Father gave Him to accomplish. Jesus relied completely on the Father to do His will, and we must do the same.

On the night of His betrayal, Jesus prayed in the garden, asking for the cup of suffering to be removed from Him.

> Abba! Father! All things are possible for You; remove this cup from Me; yet not what I will, but what You will. (Mark 14:36)

> The Spirit of the Lord is upon Me because He has anointed Me to preach the gospel to the poor; He has sent Me to proclaim release to the captives and recovery of sight to the blind, to set free those who are oppressed. (Luke 4:18)

God has given the Holy Spirit to lead you every step of the way and help you live out your calling.

> Teach me to do Your will, for You are my God; Let Your good Spirit lead me on level ground. (Psalm 143:10)

> Now may the God of hope fill you with all joy and peace in believing, so that you will abound in hope by the power of the Holy Spirit. (Romans 15:13)

> Seeing that His divine power has granted us everything pertaining to life and Godliness, through the true knowledge of

Him who called us by His own glory and excellence. And in your knowledge, self-control, and in your self-control, perseverance, and in your perseverance, godliness, and in your godliness, brotherly kindness, and in your brotherly kindness, love. (2 Peter 1:3, 6–7)

When you nourish this relationship through worship, prayer, and study good fruit is the result.

But I say, walk by the Spirit, and you will not gratify the desires of the flesh. (Galatians 5:16)

But the fruit of the Spirit is love, joy, peace, patience, kindness, goodness, faithfulness, gentleness, self-control; against such things there is no law. (Galatians 5:22–23)

If you measure the success of each day by how well you have demonstrated the fruit of the Spirit in your thoughts, beliefs, and actions, then you know that you are walking in the Spirit. The more you allow the Holy Spirit to lead your life, the more you will be transformed into the likeness of Jesus to become an effective ambassador for Christ.

Read Luke 10:41-42

How does this story contrast living from the *inside out* with living from the *outside in*? What does Jesus say to Martha about Mary?

In the hustle and bustle of life, it's all too easy to lose sight of the power and guidance that the Holy Spirit provides. Busyness, anxiety, fear, and insecurities can creep in, and it becomes clear that we have neglected our connection with the Holy Spirit. When this happens it's time to pause, reassess, and reconnect to God by choosing the better part, as Mary did.

When we are intentional about our internal life and yield to the Holy Spirit we cultivate virtues such as love, kindness, forgiveness, humility, and patience which not only enhance our relationship with God but also guide our interactions with others. This internal transformation over time allows us to navigate life's challenges with grace and dignity, and to lead by example. One thing is for certain – we can never outgrow our need for the constant dependency on the Holy Spirit.

Which Of These Areas Could You Work On?

❐ Be the same on the inside as I am on the outside.

❐ Listen to the Holy Spirit's leading.

❐ Spend time in prayer.

❐ Encourage faith in others.

What 15-minute daily practice could you implement to build the area that you identified? Use the space below to write how you plan to develop that skill.

Remember that you do not have to do this in your strength, but through the guidance and wisdom of the indwelling Holy Spirit.

> When the Spirit of truth comes, He will guide you into all truth, for He will not speak on His own authority, but whatever He hears He will speak, and He will declare to you the things that are to come. (John 16:13)

God makes this promise to all who follow Him:

> And I will give you a new heart, and a new spirit I will put within you. And I will remove the heart of stone from your flesh and give you a heart of flesh. And I will put my Spirit within you, and cause you to walk in my statutes and be careful to obey my rules. You shall dwell in the land that I gave to your fathers, and you shall be my people, and I will be your God. (Ezekiel 36:26–28)

Reflecting on the verses in Ezekiel, we can see how God's love brings about a beautiful transformation in our lives. With a new heart, a renewed spirit, and the guidance of His Holy Spirit, we can experience the fullness of life in Him.

> God is Spirit, and His worshipers must worship Him in Spirit and in truth. (John 4:24)

Read Jeremiah 29:13

What does this verse say to you? What adjustments can you make to prioritize your relationship with God?

Read Psalm 119:11

How can hiding God's word in your heart protect you from the adversary, Satan?

Walk It Out

Read Romans 8:1
How do you think God truly sees you?

_____

_____

Read Isaiah 43:1–2
How do these verses encourage you in your walk with God?

_____

_____

Read Galations 5:16–18
What are the benefits of walking in the Spirit?

_____

_____

Who encourages you in your walk with God? List each person's name and the role he or she has in your life.

But sanctify Christ as Lord in your hearts, always being ready to make a defense to everyone who asks you to give an account for the hope that is in you, yet with gentleness and reverence. (1 Peter 3:15)

I WILL LIVE CONNECTED TO THE HOLY
SPIRIT, MY POWER SOURCE FOR LIFE.

LIVING THE SURRENDERED LIFE

Trusting God

What Does It Mean To Live a Surrendered Life?

Living a surrendered life means trusting in God, yielding to His ways, and choosing to do His will.

> Be diligent to present yourself approved to God, as a workman who does not need to be ashamed, accurately handling the word of truth. (2 Timothy 2:15)

As we surrender to God, we begin to understand His purpose for our lives. We leave our old ways behind and put on the new self to walk in righteousness, holiness, and truth. We are called to know, love, and serve Christ every day to the glory of God.

> Seeing that His divine power has granted to us everything pertaining to life and Godliness, through the true knowledge of Him who called us by His own glory and excellence. (2 Peter 1:3)

> In reference to your former manner of life, you lay aside the old self, which is being corrupted in accordance with the lusts of deceit, and that you be renewed in the spirit of your mind, put on the new self,

which in the likeness of God has been created in righteousness and holiness of the truth. (Ephesians 4:22–24)

The surrendered life also puts a target on your back. When you are born into the family of God, you immediately acquire an enemy who will try to destroy you. But God is well aware of this and has already provided His armor for your use in the battle.

For example, the helmet of salvation shields your mind from the attacks of the enemy. It not only acts as a physical protection but also serves as a constant reminder of whose you are. With this helmet firmly in place, you have the assurance that you belong to the Almighty, the one who has saved and redeemed you.

> Although you were formerly alienated and hostile in mind, engaged in evil deeds, yet He has now reconciled you in His fleshly body through death, in order to present you before Him holy and blameless and beyond reproach. (Colossians 1:21–22)

Your mind is a prime battleground for the enemy. The adversary of your soul will try to influence your thought life every chance he gets to sow seeds of doubt, confusion, and lies. However, you have been bought with a price for a special purpose. Those who belong to Christ, must resist the influence and lies of the enemy. This will enable you to walk with confidence in your identity as child of God.

> Be of sober spirit, be on the alert. Your adversary, the devil, prowls around like a roaring lion, seeking someone to devour. But resist him, firm in your faith, knowing that the same experiences of suffering are being accomplished by your brethren who are in the world. (1 Peter 5:8–9)

Read Ephesians 6:12, and fill in the blanks:

For our struggle is not against _____ and _____, but against the rulers, against the powers of this dark world, and against the _____ forces of evil in the _____ _____.

If our battle is not against flesh and blood (human beings), but against the powers of this dark world and the spiritual forces of evil in the heavenly realms, what sorts of weapons can we use?

Read Ephesians 6:10-18 with a focus on verses 11 and 13

What are we told to do twice in this passage?

Read 2 Corinthians 10:3-5

How do we wage war in the battle for our minds?

Read Galatians 2:20, Colossians 3:3, and 2 Corinthians 5:17

What do these verses say about living the surrendered life?

It is critical to understand these biblical principles because they directly impact the way you think, feel, and act. By surrendering your life to Christ you allow Him to live through you, no longer relying on your own strength, but instead living by faith in the Son of God.

Read Ezekiel 36:25-26

What will God do when you yield to Him?

Only a heart of flesh can pursue the things that please God. You must know what you believe, why you believe it, and how your beliefs impact your thought life, activities, and, ultimately, your purpose. As you allow God to work in your life you will experience the transformation that only He can bring.

RIGHT BELIEFS BECOME THE ANCHOR OF YOUR SOUL.

When Jesus walked on earth He surrendered to the Father and taught us how to overcome the enemy.

> Therefore Jesus answered and was saying to them, "Truly, truly, I say to you, the Son can do nothing of Himself, unless it is something He sees the Father doing: for whatever the Father does, these things the Son also does in the same way." (John 5:19)

> I will not speak much more with you, for the ruler of the world is coming, and he has nothing in Me; but so that the world may know that I love the Father, I do exactly as the Father commanded Me. (John 14:30–31)

Read Matthew 4:1–11

List below the three temptations Jesus faced, and how He responded.

Temptation	Response

How could Satan claim to own the kingdoms of the world? Were the kingdoms of the world his to give?

> And he led Him up and showed Him all the kingdoms of the world in a moment of time. And the devil said to Him, "I will give You all this domain and its glory; *for it has been handed over to me,* and I give it to whoever I wish." (Luke 4:5–6)

It is important to understand that Satan's *ownership* is based on lies, disception, and manipulation. Unbelievers are blinded by Satan's influence and, therefore, cannot submit to God's righteousness.

> By this the children of God and the children of the devil are obvious: anyone who does not practice righteousness is not of God, nor the one who does not love his brother. (1 John 3:10)

> The prophet Jeremiah said, "The heart is more deceitful than all else and is desperately sick; Who can understand it?" (Jeremiah 17:9)

As believers, we have the power to stand against the wiles of the enemy. Ephesians 6 reminds us of this truth. The battles we face are not against mere human beings, but against the spiritual forces of darkness. When we trust in Jesus, we have victory over these powers. When faced with temptation, Jesus responded with the Truth. We must do the same.

> You dear children, are from God and have overcome them, because the one who is in you is greater than the one who is in the world. (1 John 4:4)

The presence of God's Spirit within us gives us the power to overcome the schemes and attacks of the enemy. Jesus has conquered the world, and as His children, we share in that victory.

Read Ephesians 2:1–3, 1 Corinthians 2:14, Romans 8:5–8, and 2 Corinthians 4:4

Note the contrasts between nonbelievers and believers.

This battle requires you to remain vigilant about what you allow into your mind and heart. We cannot afford to let Satan's influence infiltrate our thoughts and actions. When you come face to face with an attack from the evil one, do not retreat. Arm yourself with the most powerful weapon of all – the Word of God. Let the truth of the Word of God cut through the darkness bringing light to the path before you to defeat the enemy.

This is why it is so important to study the Bible with diligence, for within its pages you will find the strength to use the sword of the Spirit, the—Word of God—in every battle against the forces of darkness.

Read Proverbs 4:23

Why is it so important to guard your heart?

Read Revelation 12:11

How are the people of God able to triumph over the enemy?

When you encounter an attack from the evil one, immediately go to the Bible for the Truth. The Sword of the Spirit—another piece of God's armor—is the Word of God. This offensive weapon of Truth unmasks the enemy's lies.

WHAT WE BELIEVE TO BE TRUE MATTERS.

> My son (daughter), give attention to my words; incline your ear to my sayings. Do not let them depart from your sight; keep them in the midst of your heart. For they are life to those who find them and health to all their body. Watch over your heart with all diligence, for from it flow the springs of life. (Proverbs 4:20–23)

We are completely reliant on the Spirit of God to instruct us in the Truth and guide us on the correct path. Let us boldly declare our victory in Jesus.

Read Colossians 1:21–23

What do these verses say about the surrendered life?

When your life is surrendered to God, your thoughts and actions are aligned to God's plumb line, and you remain firmly established and steadfast and not easily moved away from the hope of the gospel. However, that surrender is not a one-time event; we must daily surrender our hearts and minds to God. After all, the enemy never takes a day off.

Read Philippians 2:12–13

Why do you think Paul instructs us to work out our salvation with fear and trembling?

Read 1 Peter 5:8–9

What is Peter's word of warning to those who try to walk out their faith in the surrounding culture? Are they alone in their efforts? Who is trying to destroy them?

> For the gate is small and the way is narrow that leads to life, and there are few who find it. (Matthew 7:14)

> I will keep watch over my ways so that I do not sin with my tongue; I will guard my mouth as with a muzzle while the wicked are in my presence. I was mute and silent, I refrained even from good, and my sorrow grew worse. My heart was hot within me, while I was musing the fire burned; then I spoke with my tongue: "Lord, let me know my end, and what is the extent of my days; let me know how transient I am." (Psalm 39:1–4)

> I hold fast my righteousness and will not let it go. My heart does not reproach any of my days. (Job 27:6)

Read Deuteronomy 8:1–5

What did Moses instruct the Israelites to do before entering into the Promised Land?

Jesus said, "If you love me keep my commandments." John 14:15

Obedience to God's commands keeps us on the narrow path and in alignment with His plumb line. As we ask the Holy Spirit for wisdom and discernment, He shows us how to apply God's commands to our lives.

> His divine power has given us everything we need for a godly life through our knowledge of Him who called us by His own glory and goodness. For by these He has granted to us His precious and magnificent promises, so that by them you may become partakers of the divine nature, having escaped the corruption that is in the world by lust. (2 Peter 1:3–4)

As long as you live on this earth, your new nature in Christ and your old sinful nature will be at war with each other. But as you surrender daily and allow the Holy Spirit to lead you, you will increasingly die to yourself and be made alive in Christ Jesus.

Read Deuteronomy 20:19–20

We have both fruitful and unfruitful trees in our lives. We must nourish the fruitful trees, but what do we do with the unfruitful trees? We cut them down and use them to build a bulwark against the enemy. What does this mean in practical terms?

Unfruitful trees are those things in our lives that are not pleasing to God. For example, when the unfruitful trees of doubt and fear crop up in your life, the Holy Spirit helps you recognize them as lies from the enemy. Once you cut them down, the enemy is exposed, and those felled trees become a bulwark (a wall or fortress) from which to fight the lies of the enemy.

Jesus fought the enemy with the Word of God, and when we follow His example, the enemy must flee. Walking in obedience will rarely be easy, but the Holy Spirit gives us what we need to follow God's commands.

GOD DOES NOT PROVIDE A WAY TO IMPROVE US, HE PROVIDES A WAY TO RESTORE US.

This is what the Lord said to Joshua: "Be strong and very courageous. Be careful to obey all the law my servant Moses gave you, do not turn from it to the right or to the left, that you may be successful wherever you go. Do not let this Book of the Law depart from your mouth; meditate on it day and night, so that you may be careful to do everything written in it. Then you will be prosperous and successful." (Joshua 1:7–8)

Read Psalm 119:25-32

After meditating on these eight verses, how can you have a *heart set free* by the Lord?

Jesus said to Jewish believers, "If you hold to my teaching, then you are really my disciples. Then you will know the truth, and the truth will set you free." (John 8:31–32)

When you study what the Bible teaches, you equip yourself to give an answer for the truth that lies within you. You will not only be able to defend what you believe but also explain why you believe it. Defending the faith is known as *Christian apologetics*.

> Be diligent to present yourself approved to God as a worker who does not need to be ashamed, accurately handling the word of truth. (2 Timothy 2:15)

As our society grows darker and darker, sins that were once hidden are now out in the open and celebrated in our communities, schools, and even churches.

> But realize this, that in the last days difficult times will come. For men will be lovers of self, lovers of money, boastful, arrogant,

revilers, disobedient to parents, ungrateful, unholy, unloving, irreconcilable, malicious gossips, without self-control, brutal, haters of good, treacherous, reckless, conceited, lovers of pleasure rather than lovers of God. (2 Timothy 3:1–5)

How do we stand against this growing unrighteousness? To be an overcomer, you must commit to studying God's word and allowing the Holy Spirit to lead and guide you in all truth. Pray daily for spiritual discernment to walk in the righteousness that comes through faith in Jesus alone.

All Scripture is inspired by God and profitable for teaching, for reproof, for correction, for training in righteousness so that the man of God may be adequate, equipped for every good work. (2 Timothy 3:16–17)

As we look to God to lead us, we can trust that He will order our steps. When things around us seem to be out of control, we can trust in God's Sovereignty—His authority and power to work all things out according to His purpose and will. Trust Him to guide you in all things as you live out the surrendered life.

I HAVE SAID THESE THINGS TO YOU,
THAT IN ME YOU MAY HAVE PEACE.
IN THE WORLD, YOU WILL HAVE TRIBULATION.
BUT TAKE HEART; I HAVE
OVERCOME THE WORLD.
(JOHN 16:33)

Walk It Out

We can have confidence that God will direct our paths when we look to Him for direction. We can take comfort in the knowledge that God is in charge of everything when life seems chaotic. He has the utmost power and control to make sure that everything happens according to what He wants and intends.

> So Jesus was saying to those Jews who had believed Him, "If you continue in My word, then you are truly My disciples." (John 8:31–32).

As you study the Bible and continue to live a life of submission to Christ, how can you rely on Him to guide you in every area of your life?

_____

_____

_____

_____

_____

How will you prepare to defend your beliefs as stated in 2 Timothy 2:15?

_____

_____

_____

_____

_____

THE PATH TO SUCCESS

LESSON 5

Aligning with God's Purpose

Think for a moment about why God created you. What do you think His purpose is for your life?

An architect's blueprints for a structure reflect the building's intended purpose. For example, the blueprints for a hospital, a museum, or a residence may share common features, but each one is uniquely designed for a specific purpose. Similarly, God, the Sovereign Architect of His creation, shows us what we have in common, but He designs each of us for a unique purpose.

How does this relate to success? First, think about the ways that the world defines success. Do you think a Christian can be faithful and successful at the same time?

When you stand before God at the end of your life, do you think He will say, "Wow, excellent work to earn that promotion?" or "I'm so proud you were able to close that million-dollar deal?"

Jesus gave us an example to follow, and our Heavenly Father will probably ask us questions like: "How well did you know my Son?" "How did you treat your family?" "How did you nurture your relationships?" "Were you a good steward with your time, talent, and treasure?" and "Did you serve others or did you expect them to serve you?"

Though the world measures success by power and prosperity, God measures success differently for His children. From God's perspective, success means walking *His* way. As the Holy Spirit reveals God's heart to us, we learn to walk in obedience as we follow Him.

SUCCESS IS THE PROGRESSIVE REALIZATION OF WHO GOD CREATED YOU TO BE, AND THEN FAITHFULLY DOING WHAT HE HAS CALLED YOU TO DO.

Now, Israel, what does the Lord your God require from you, but to fear the Lord your God, to walk in all His ways and love Him, and to serve the Lord your God with all your heart and with all your soul. (Deuteronomy 10:12)

You will seek Me and find Me when you search for Me with all your heart. (Jeremiah 29:13)

Search me, O God, and know my heart; put me to the test and know my anxious thoughts; and see if there is any hurtful way in me and lead me in the everlasting way. (Psalm 139:23–24)

His Master replied, "Well done, good and faithful servant! You have been faithful with a few things; I will put you in charge of many things. Come and share your master's happiness!" (Matthew 25:21)

How we long to hear the Father say those words to us when one day, we see Him face to face.

Read John 6:27 and Matthew 4:4

For what does God say we should labor?

Read the following Scripture passages Malachi 3:16–18, 2 Peter 2:5–9, Psalm 31:23–24, Romans 1:17–19, 1 Thessalonians 5:5–9, Proverbs 13:1–5, and Matthew 24:45–51 List the characteristics of the unfaithful children of the world and those of the faithful children of God. Note the contrasts.

Unfaithful Children of the World	Faithful Children of God

What can the faithful expect as a reward for their righteousness and obedience?

BE STRONG AND COURAGEOUS.

After God had miraculously delivered the Israelites from Egypt, the people were preparing to enter the Promised Land. But first, the Lord gave their leader, Joshua, a charge. This account shows true success from God's perspective.

As you read the following passage, underline each occurrence of God saying to Joshua, *"Be strong and courageous."* Then, double underline what God told the Israelites to be careful to do. Finally, highlight what the result would be.

> God told Joshua, "Be strong and courageous because you will lead these people to inherit the land I swore to their forefathers to give them. Be strong and very courageous. Be careful to obey all the law my servant Moses gave you; do not turn from it to the right or to the left, that you may be successful wherever you go. Do not let this Book of the Law depart from your mouth; meditate on it day and night, so that you may be careful to do everything written in it. Then you will be prosperous and successful. Have I not commanded you? Be strong and courageous. Do not be terrified; do not be discouraged, for the Lord your God will be with you wherever you go." (Joshua 1:6–9)

> Later, Joshua proclaimed to the people, "Now fear the Lord and serve Him with all faithfulness. Throw away the gods your forefathers worshiped beyond the River and in Egypt and serve the Lord. But if serving the Lord seems undesirable to you, then choose for yourselves this day whom you will serve, whether the gods your forefathers served beyond the River, or the gods of the Amorites, in whose land you are living. But as for me and my household, we will serve the Lord." (Joshua 24:14–15)

Like the ancient Israelites, you will either be influenced by the world or by God's word. You must choose between the two pathways: one leads to LIFE; the other leads to destruction.

> Enter through the narrow gate; for the gate is wide and the way is broad that leads to destruction, and there are many who enter through it. For the gate is narrow and the way is constricted that leads to life, and there are few who find it. (Matthew 7:13–14)

If you take to heart the principle found in Joshua 1:8, *do not let this Book of the Law depart from your mouth; meditate on it day and night, so that you may be careful to do everything written in it*, the Truth of God's word will lead you on the path of life.

> All Scripture is breathed out by God and profitable for teaching, for reproof, for correction, and for training in righteousness, that

the man of God may be complete, equipped for every good work. (2 Timothy 3:16–17)

"Come, follow Me," Jesus said, "and I will make you fishers of men." Matthew 4:19

What do you think God's intended purpose for humanity is?

God's purpose for humanity has always been that we truly know Him. He desires a loving relationship with us. He desires us to walk in His ways and develop righteous character. He desires that we grow in the grace and knowledge of Him so that His life is seen in all that we say and do. He desires that we would be His witnesses in the earth.

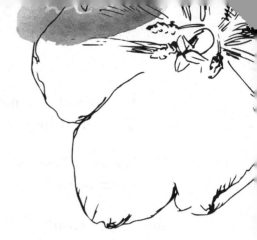

Walk It Out

God is raising a great company of women to **shine the light of Christ into the darkness:**

- Women who seek to know God on a deeper level.

- Women who prioritize prayer and live a life that reflects God's presence in all that they say and do.

- Women who contend for their homes, their children, their families, and their communities.

- Women who understand the purpose of bringing the kingdom of God into every area of their lives and becoming a positive witness for Christ. This is the *true* path to success.

Do you see yourself in this great company of women? What are you doing?

_____

_____

_____

_____

_____

_____

_____

_____

_____

_____

_____

ABIDING IN THE TRUE VINE

Nurturing Faith for a Fruitful Life

Did you know that God has given you everything you need to live a godly life? That's right. Everything. As you surrender your life to Jesus and yield to the Holy Spirit, you will begin to demonstrate characteristics that mark the life of the true Christian—the fruit of the Spirit.

> But the fruit of the Spirit is love, joy, peace, patience, kindness, goodness, faithfulness, gentleness and self-control. (Galatians 5:22–23)

Fruitfulness in the Christian life is not the result of human achievement, but the result of a new life in Jesus Christ.

Just before Jesus was crucified, He gave the beautiful metaphor of the True Vine as an encouragement to His followers. He would not leave them or forsake them but would continue to nourish and sustain them.

> I am the True Vine, and My Father is the vinedresser. Every branch in Me that does not bear fruit, He takes away; and every branch that bears fruit, He prunes it so that it may bear more fruit. You are already clean because of the word which I have spoken to you. Remain in Me and I in you. Just as the branch cannot bear fruit of itself but must remain in the vine, so neither can you unless

you remain in Me. I am the vine, you are the branches; the one who remains in Me, and I in him bears much fruit, for apart from Me you can do nothing. (John 15:1–5)

Just as the roots and trunk of the grapevine provide the nourishment needed to produce fruit, our fruitfulness depends on our connection to the True Vine. As we abide in Christ, we produce good fruit that will last.

When difficulties come, you can have faith in God's boundless love and trust in His ability to turn any situation into something good.

And we know that God causes all things to work together for good to those who love God, to those who are called according to His purpose. (Romans 8:28)

In Genesis 16:7–13, God revealed Himself to Hagar as EL ROI, the God who sees. This divine encounter took place when Hagar, who was pregnant with Abraham's child, fled from her mistress Sarah due to mistreatment. Alone and distressed in the desert, an angel of the Lord found Hagar by a spring of water. The angel spoke to her and told her to return to her mistress and submit to her authority. But in this moment, God also revealed His character to Hagar, assuring her that He sees her and knows her circumstances.

EL ROI portrays God's nature as a powerful and caring Shepherd. Just as a shepherd diligently keeps watch over his flock, God watches over His children. He never loses sight of us, even in the midst of our trials and challenges.

Understanding God's character as EL ROI brings comfort and confidence. It reminds us that we are not alone in our battles. He sees our struggles, our pain, and our fears. Knowing this, we can trust that He is with us, leading and protecting us through every obstacle we face.

Life is filled with difficulties, some of which we have no control over. However, we have the power to choose how we respond to these situations. Running the race set before us requires perseverance and faith. When we face challenges, we can look to God as EL ROI, knowing that He sees us and is present in our lives.

Therefore, since we also have such a great cloud of witnesses surrounding us, let us also lay aside every encumbrance and the sin which so easily entangles us, and let's run with endurance the race that is set before us. (Hebrews 12:1)

Paul writes, I have fought the good fight, I have finished the course, I have kept the faith. (2 Timothy 4:7)

Sometimes when we face difficulties, it is because we have not yet renewed our minds in certain areas. When confronted with challenge, it is important to assess your beliefs as well as your reactions to certain situations.

We live in an increasingly reactive culture. As tempers flare, riots ensue. And a steady stream of vitriol on social media can pull us in if we aren't careful.

If we feel defensive, fearful, misrepresented, or misunderstood, we might be inclined to respond negatively when we encounter strong emotions. It's crucial to realize that even in challenging situations, we always have the opportunity to express the truth with kindness. When we hold genuine passion for something, intense reactions can occur.

What things provoke a reaction in you?

What does God's word say about these things? Are you responding correctly?

In situations like these, it may be helpful to...

Pause
When faced with strong emotions, its helpful to pause before responding. This helps you to collect your thoughts, pray, and allow the Holy Spirit to flow through you. This will help you to respond with more clarity and avoid reactive responses that may harm the conversation.

Recognize Your Emotions
Take a step back and identify the emotions you are experiencing. Acknowledge any defensiveness, fear, or feeling of being misrepresented. Understanding and accepting your emotions will help you to respond more effectively.

Practice Self-awareness

Be mindful of how your own emotions and biases may be influencing your perspective and any distortions in your thinking that may not be aligned with God's truth.

Seek to Understand

Instead of immediately defending your point of view, try to understand the other person's perspective. Listen actively, show empathy, and ask questions to gain a deeper understanding. This will foster a more constructive conversation and show that you truly value their perspective.

Communicate Respectfully

Express the truth with kindness and respect, even in challenging situations. Choose your words carefully and keep the tone of the conversation positive and constructive. This will show the other person that you value and respect them even when you have a different point of view.

> But speaking the truth in love, we are to grow up in all aspects unto Him who is the head, even Christ. (Ephesians 4:15)

> The heart of the righteous ponders how to answer, but the mouth of the wicked pours out evil things. (Proverbs 15:28)

> This you know, my beloved brethren. But everyone must be quick to hear, slow to speak, and slow to anger. (James 1:19)

> Let no unwholesome word proceed from your mouth, but only such a word as is good for edification according to the need of the moment, so that it will give grace to those who hear. (Ephesians 4:29)

Use difficult situations as an opportunity for personal and spiritual growth. Reflect on what you can learn from the experience, whether it's improving your communication skills, challenging your own assumptions or biases, or finding better ways to handle conflict in the future.

Read Philippians 2:3

What is the admonition in this passage? Is this hard for you? If so, why?

Read Philippians 4:13 and Psalms 138:8

What encouragement so you find in these passages?

> And the Lord said to Paul in the night by a vision, "Do not be afraid any longer, but go on speaking and do not be silent." (Acts 18:9)

> And do not fear their intimidation, and do not be troubled, but sanctify Christ as Lord in your hearts, always being ready to make a defense to everyone who asks you to give an account for the hope that is in you, yet with gentleness and reverence. (1 Peter 3:14–16)

> Like apples of gold in settings of silver is a word spoken in right circumstances. (Proverbs 25:11)

It's helpful to keep a prayer a journal and document how the Holy Spirit speaks to your heart. Meditating on Psalm 139 at the end of your day will help to create an intimate dialogue with God as He speaks truth to your heart and guides you on your faith journey. You are His daughter; The Good Shepherd loves you and wants to support your spiritual growth in righteousness. This daily practice will help you to be a reflection of Gods light and love in your relationships and course correct when needed.

> Search me, O God, and know my heart; try me and know my anxious thoughts; and see if there be any hurtful way in me; and lead me in the everlasting way."Psalm 139:23–24

- Lord, was there anything I did today that displeased You?
- Did I miss anything while interacting with the people around me?

There may be times when you stumble and fall, when you succumb to sin and wander off the path. But fear not, for God is a forgiving and merciful Father. When you turn to Him with a repentant heart, He is ready to forgive you and cleanse you from your sin. He is eager to release you from the chains of guilt and shame and to restore you into a close relationship with Him.

> If we confess our sins, He is faithful and righteous to forgive us our sins and to cleanse us from all unrighteousness. (1 John 1:9)

> The Law came in so that the transgression would increase; but where sin increased, grace abounded all the more, so that, as sin reigned in death even so grace would reign through righteousness to eternal life through Jesus Christ our Lord. (Romans 5:20–21)

Read Proverbs 4:25

How does this verse help when you are in challenging or uncertain situations?

> Brethren, I do not regard myself as having taken hold of it yet; but one thing I do: forgetting what lies behind and reaching forward to what lies ahead, I press on toward the goal for the prize of the upward call of God in Christ Jesus. (Philippians 3:13–14)

When you face challenges and struggles, it is important to evaluate your responses. Are your responses proactive or reactive?

To be *proactive* is to anticipate what lies ahead and to eliminate the things that create obstacles and challenges before they occur. This response keeps you from a victim mentality.

To be *reactive* is to respond to obstacles and challenges in the moment, before thinking them through. This response can sabotage the situation.

Proactive people set goals and create plans to achieve them. Reactive people are more likely to wait for an opportunity to present itself before taking any action.

We need to learn to let go and stop dwelling on past mistakes and regrets so that we are not trapped in a cycle of negativity. Instead, practice forgiveness toward yourself and others. Holding on to the past prevents you from moving forward and experiencing freedom and growth. Invite the Holy Spirit to help you to identify and release any negative emotions.

My Own Journey

Over twenty years ago, I experienced a situation that involved someone dear to my heart. There was potential for danger and loss, the situation was out of my control. I felt helpless and wondered why God would allow this terrible thing to happen. I experienced tremendous fear for this person, and started to feel depressed. I felt like there was nothing I could do, and hopelessness started to take over.

I had learned about proactive and reactive responses, which helped me to think about how to handle this situation. I realized that my initial response was driven by fear. Once I understood that, I shifted my focus on God's truth and sought guidance from Him.

As I looked to the Lord for wisdom to manage my fear and my sense of helplessness, I felt the Holy Spirit giving me wisdom in the form of a question: "What can you control in this situation?" I had to reply, "Nothing Lord." Another bit of wisdom from Him: "What then are you able to do?" I responded, "The only thing that I can do is pray." When I realized that prayer was the most powerful thing I could do, I found peace and trusted that the Lord would be faithful, even when I didn't understand why it was happening.

In this situation, I had to cling to *EL ROI*, the God who sees everything. God reminded me that He was aware of the actions of the person I deeply cared about. I had to let go of my own desires and trust that God's plan would guide both of us toward something beneficial and for His glory.

GOD IS FAITHFUL.

I went from feeling afraid and hopeless to taking the positive actions of praying and trusting in God. This helped me to stay strong for the next ten years until the person I cared about was rescued from the situation. Throughout those years, God reassured me that He was always with me and my loved one. I found great comfort in reading the Bible and holding onto God's promises while I waited for my prayers to be answered. My belief in God's faithfulness kept me going during that difficult time. With God's help, I was able to replace my negative feelings of fear, hopelessness, and depression with trust, faith, and obedience. To God be all glory.

What About You?

Think about areas where you struggle, or experience fear, worry, or sadness. Which ones would you like to gain the mind of Christ and surrender to the Lord?

It's not easy, but there is hope. God is there for you to help you bring the fruit of righteousness even in the midst of difficulties. Underline in the verse below what God desires to give to those who mourn in Zion.

> To grant to those who mourn in Zion, giving them a garland instead of ashes, the oil of gladness instead of mourning, the mantle of praise instead of a spirit of fainting. So they will be called oaks of righteousness, the planting of the Lord, that He may be glorified. (Isaiah 61:3)

> Having been filled with the fruit of righteousness which comes through Jesus Christ, to the glory and praise of God. (Philippians 1:11)

When we surrender our life to Christ and allow His spirit to work in us we can be vessels through which God's righteousness and love can be displayed to others. This exchange is meant to transform us into strong and steadfast women, likened to *"oaks of righteousness,"* which are firmly planted and rooted in God's righteousness.

Key Steps for Responding to Challenging Situations

1. **Self-Awareness.** Take a moment to reflect on the challenging situation you are experiencing. What is happening?

    - What is beyond your control?

    - What actions or steps can you take in this particular situation?

    - What negative emotions or behaviors are you currently experiencing?

   Be honest and open with yourself, as this is essential for personal development. Examples of negative emotions include are anger, uncertainty about yourself, resentment, fear, or unproductive habits. Acknowledge that these emotions are not conducive to walking by faith.

2. **Seek Divine Help.** Take a moment to direct your attention toward God and pray. Invite Him to help you recognize your need for His wisdom, strength, and guidance.

    - What message is God conveying to your innermost being?

    - What Bible verses specifically address the things you are concerned about?

3. **God's Pruning.** Jesus said, "every branch that does not bear fruit He prunes so that it may bear more fruit" (John 15:2).

   Spiritual pruning involves getting rid of anything that hinders our spiritual development and prevents us from attaining inner peace and righteousness.

    - Which negative emotions are currently affecting your peace of mind?

- Is God showing you any sin that He wants you to bring to Him? If so, confess it immediately. 1 John 1:9 says that He is faithful and just to forgive us of our sin, and cleanse us from all unrighteousness.

4. **Prayer and Surrender.** When you pray to God about these things, always remember that He is readily available to embrace you and to purify you from any wrongdoing or negative thoughts.

One aspect of the healing journey involves allowing the Lord to free you from guilt or shame associated with the things that you are giving to Him. He loves you and will always be available to meet you whenever you come to Him and ask for His help.

As you surrender to God, envision yourself being completely purified and forgiven by Him. Actively reflecting on the truths you have received through this process will help you overcome the reoccurrence of negative influences in your life. Put on the full armor of God and stand as you gain the victory over your thoughts and emotions.

5. **Practice Gratitude.** Cultivate an attitude of gratitude, focusing on the blessings and lessons you have received despite the challenging experience you are going through. Meditate on the unwavering kindness and goodness of God. As you patiently wait for the answers to your prayers, this will provide you with strength and courage.

The definition of COURAGE from Noah Webster's 1828 dictionary: Bravery; intrepidity; that quality of mind which enables men to encounter danger and difficulties with firmness, or without fear or depression of spirits; valor; boldness; resolution. It is a constituent part of fortitude; but fortitude implies patience to bear continued suffering.

6. **Spiritual Fruit.** This is where the transformation happens. When you walk by faith and surrender your negative thinking, you exchange it for the fruit of the Holy Spirit. The outcome of having the Spirit within you is characterized by "love, joy, peace, patience, kindness, goodness, faithfulness, gentleness, and self-control; against such things there is no law." (Galatians 5:22–23).

And you will know the truth, and the truth will make you free. (John 8:32)

The journey from pruning to cultivating is often challenging but immensely rewarding. By trusting in the process and actively participating in the transformation, we let God prune away the negative fruit and cultivate righteous fruit in its place.

Take courage; change takes time, patience, and consistency. These steps will help you to identify the areas you need to improve, shield you from falling victim to the schemes of the enemy, and enable you to triumph over your negative thoughts and sinful desires. Keep your connection with God strong, reach out for help from others, and don't forget to celebrate every achievement and progress you make on your journey.

Read Romans 7:22–25; 8:2; 12: 1–2, and Jeremiah 29:12–13

Write your impressions from these verses.

> Blessed be the God and Father of our Lord Jesus Christ, the Father of mercies and God of all comfort, who comforts us in all of our affliction so that we will be able to comfort those who are in any affliction with which we ourselves are comforted by God. For just as the sufferings of Christ are ours in abundance, so also our comfort is abundant through Christ. (2 Corinthians 1:3–5)

Life is indeed fragile and full of challenges, heartaches, and difficulties. It is during these times that your faith and your focus on God become crucial. God, the Author and Finisher of your faith, is always with you, whether you are on the mountaintops of joy or in the valley of despair.

God promises to provide you with the strength and guidance you need to navigate all of life's uncertainties. You can hold on to the hope and peace that comes from knowing that He is walking beside you every step of the way. With Jesus Christ as your Lord and Savior, you can confidently face whatever challenges come your way.

> Therefore, as you have received Christ Jesus the Lord, so walk in Him, having been firmly rooted and now being built up in Him and established in your faith, just as you were instructed, and overflowing with gratitude. (Colossians 2:6–7)

Abiding In Christ

This is the key to experiencing true peace, joy, and fulfillment in life. As you abide in Jesus, your decisions are guided by His word, and your desires are transformed to reflect His heart.

> For in Him we live and move and exist. (Acts 17:28)

> You will make known to me the path of life; in Your presence is fullness of joy; in Your right hand are pleasures forever. (Psalm 16:11)

> But we all, with unveiled face, beholding as in a mirror the glory of the Lord, are being transformed into the same image from glory to glory, just as from the Lord, the Spirit. (2 Corinthians 3:18)

Walk It Out

In God's presence, you'll find the peace, comfort, and strength to overcome any challenge. When you're feeling trapped in your emotions or actions, refer back to **the steps for responding to challenging situations**.

> Seeing that His divine power has granted to us everything pertaining to life and Godliness, through the true knowledge of Him who called us by His own glory and excellence. (2 Peter 1:3)

What did the Holy Spirit bring to your mind as you worked through this lesson?

_____

_____

_____

_____

_____

_____

_____

What is He asking you to do?

_____

_____

_____

_____

_____

_____

_____

BLUEPRINTS OF GRACE

God's Design for Your Life

God is our Creator and the Sovereign Architect of our lives. He has designed a unique blueprint for each person. As we follow our individual blueprints and walk in the power of the Spirit, we can build a life aligned with God's plumb line.

> For we are His workmanship, created in Christ Jesus for good works, which God prepared beforehand so that we would walk in them. (Ephesians 2:10)

Your talents, gifts, passions, strengths, weaknesses, temperament, and convictions are all part of God's design. Even your fingerprints express your one-of-a-kind existence.

Which of your characteristics do you consider particularly unique to you?

As you view yourself from God's blueprint of grace, you will begin to value the person He has created you to be. Your self-concept will be defined by God and not by the world, other people, or your untrustworthy emotions. Once you grasp this truth, you will be free to fully experience His workmanship in you and express His intended purpose for your life.

A biblical self-concept helps you answer questions such as, *Who Am I? Why Am I here? What is My Purpose? How Can I Have Influence?*

From the beginning, God has had a plan for your life. You are His masterpiece.

> For You formed my inward parts; You wove me in my mother's womb. I will give thanks to You, for I am fearfully and wonderfully made; wonderful are Your works, and my soul knows it very well. My frame was not hidden from You, when I was made in secret, and skillfully wrought in the depths of the earth; Your eyes have seen my unformed substance; and in Your book were all written the days that were ordained for me, when as yet there was not one of them. (Psalm 139:13-16)

What significance is placed on the heart of the inner man in the following passages and what are the results?

Proverbs 4:23

Matthew 15:18

Romans 10:10

Ephesians 3:16

2 Corinthians 3:3

1 Samuel 16:7

Luke 6:45

The world looks at outward appearances to define beauty, success, and value. How would you say that beauty is defined in advertisements, television, movies, and on social media?

Let's compare the way the world defines beauty with the way the Bible defines it.

The media focuses on the external, suggesting that this narrow definition of beauty is something to attain. Young girls, in particular, suffer from negative self-concepts as they strive to meet these unrealistic standards. The obsession with appearance has resulted in alarming rates of eating disorders, body dysmorphias, and self-harm. Cosmetic surgery has also skyrocketed, exposing the deep dissatisfaction plaguing women today.

The pursuit of media-defined perfection is a never-ending pit of darkness. Perfection is unattainable, leaving us constantly longing for what we do not have. After graduating from high school, I studied to become a cosmetologist. In my salon career, I witnessed women desperately seeking to change their natural features, be it straightening curly hair or curling straight hair. This raises the question – why do we reject what we have been given? What if we embraced our uniqueness, recognizing that we are a unique design by God?

True beauty, as defined by God, goes beyond outward appearances. It is not a shallow measure based on physical attributes. It is found in a woman's character and her relationship with God. It is about having a heart that is humble and displays virtues such as kindness, love, and compassion toward others.

So, let us reject the shallow measure of beauty dictated by society and instead nurture the virtues and qualities that define our true worth. It is time to redefine beauty in alignment with God's definition and find strength, confidence, and inspiration as we represent this true reflection of beauty to the world around us.

> Strength and dignity are her clothing, and she smiles at the future, she opens her mouth with wisdom, and the teaching of kindness is on her tongue. Charm is deceitful and beauty is vain, but a woman who fears the Lord, she shall be praised. (Proverbs 31:25–26, 30)

> You will also be a crown of beauty in the hand of the Lord, and a royal diadem in the hand of your God. (Isaiah 62:3)

Your adornment must not be merely the external braiding the hair, and wearing gold jewelry, or putting on dresses; but let it be the hidden person of the heart, with the imperishable quality of a gentle and quiet spirit, which is precious in the sight of God. (1 Peter 3:3–4)

For God sees not as man sees, for man looks at the outward appearance, but the Lord looks at the heart. (1 Samuel 16:7)

How lovely on the mountains are the feet of him who brings good news, who announces peace and brings good news of happiness, who announces salvation, and says to Zion, "Your God reigns!" (Isaiah 52:7)

And God saw all that He had made, and behold, it was very good. (Genesis 1:31)

1. How do you define true worth and beauty in a world that promotes shallow measures of beauty?

2. How can we nurture the virtues and qualities that reflect our true worth and beauty, as opposed to the world's standards?

3. How can we balance external adornment with the cultivation of a gentle and quiet spirit that is precious in the sight of God?

4. How can we embody the qualities of strength, dignity, wisdom, and kindness in our daily lives as a reflection of true beauty?

Read Ephesians 2:10, Exodus 9:16, and 1 Peter 2:9

1. How does the idea of being created for good works make you feel about your purpose in life?

2. In what ways does God's declaration of purpose for His people in Exodus and Peter's letter impact how you see yourself and your role in the world?

3. How can you align your experiences, gifts, and talents to fulfill the purposes God had declared over His people?

You are created for a specific purpose, which is to do good works and to proclaim God's power and glory. God has chosen and called His people to be a light in the world to declare His praises and to demonstrate His power.

AS YOU REFLECT ON WHAT GOD SAYS IS TRUE,
YOU WILL UNCOVER YOUR INDIVIDUALITY
AND BEGIN TO BLOSSOM INTO THE
WOMAN HE HAS CALLED YOU TO BE.

1. How does this give you a sense of significance and responsibility, knowing that you are created with a divine purpose?

2. How can you live in a way that reflects God's character and actively seek out opportunities to share His greatness in your sphere of influence?

How Do You Currently Spend Your Time?

Do your activities reflect your God-given gifts and talents? Do they bring you a sense of fulfillment and purpose? Or are you just filling your days with empty pursuits?

Do Your Activities Connect With Your Purpose?

If not, think about why you continue to spend your time that way. Are you seeking validation from others? Are you trapped in a comfort zone? Are you living up to your true potential?

What actions do you need to take to align your gifts and talents with your purpose?

As you realign your gifts and talents with your God-given design and purpose, a wonderful transformation awaits you. You will find yourself equipped with the ability to make choices guided by conscience, conviction, and a true sense of mission, all aligned with your true purpose. This insight will empower you to discern which activities truly resonate, while identifying those that may prove to be a waste of your precious time.

> For those who He foreknew He also predestined to be conformed to the image of His Son, in order that He might be the firstborn among many brothers. (Romans 8:29)

> He has told you, O man, what is good; and what does the Lord require of you but to do justice, and to love kindness, and to walk humbly with your God. (Micah 6:8)

> So, whether you eat or drink, or whatever you do, do all for the glory of God. (1 Corinthians 10:31)

Read 2 Corinthians 5:17, Ephesians 2:8; 4:24, and John 3:3–6

Describe how God sees you.

Walk It Out

Christian sister, as a woman called by God, it is important to hold fast to these truths:

- You have unique qualities that you must share with others.
- You are fearfully and wonderfully made.
- You can trust that God has a plan and purpose for your life.
- You are designed to have a transformational impact on the people around you and even on the world.
- You must keep seeking God to fulfill your life's mission and calling.

Embracing these truths will empower you to walk confidently in your faith and fulfill the purpose God has for your life. Keep these truths close to your heart as you continue on your journey of faith for your life. Here are some questions to reflect on to integrate God's blueprint of grace into your life:

1. How can I utilize my unique qualities to share God's love and grace with others?
2. In what ways can I trust in God's plan and purpose for my life despite challenges or uncertainties?
3. What steps can I take to have a transformational impact on the people around me and in the world, in alignment with God's will?
4. How can I consistently seek God to fulfill my life's mission and calling, staying open to His guidance and wisdom?

By pondering these questions and seeking God's guidance, you can align your life with His grace and purpose, fulfilling the unique role He has for you as a woman who is called by God.

GOD IS SOVEREIGN

His Ways Are Not Our Ways

As we observe the crises that America is experiencing, we must remember that these struggles are not new. The Old Testament prophet Habakkuk experienced the same issues and frustrations as he looked for answers. Habakkuk's experience provides a powerful lesson for us today. The prophet struggled with doubts, and he asked the Lord why He allowed terrible things to happen to His people, the Israelites, and why the ungodly were not being judged.

Read the book of Habakkuk

Write the verses that address Habakkuk's issues. The first question provides an example.

1. Habakkuk's struggle with doubt:
   Example: Habakkuk 1:2: "How long will You not hear me when I cry out and not help me?"

2. God's sovereignty: evil exists, but God is still in control:

3. Hope in God alone:

4. Habakkuk's progress from doubt to confidence in God:

Read Habakkuk 1:2-3, 12-13, 17

Make a list of Habakkuk's questions.

Habakkuk was troubled by the apparent inaction of the Lord, and he questioned why God allows violence and injustice to prevail and why He does not intervene to save His people. Habakkuk wondered why God allows the wicked to prosper and the righteous to suffer. Many are the cries of those who are persecuted and who are desperate for God's intervention and salvation

What did God say in response to Habakkuk's questions?

God patiently answered the prophet's questions and reminded Habakkuk of His faithfulness throughout the generations. God assures us that He is in control and will bring about justice in His own time.

This demonstrates for us too that God is actively working behind the scenes even when we don't see evidence. God is calling us to have faith in His plan and to trust that He will ultimately balance the scales and provide deliverance.

God invites us to come before His Throne of Grace.

> Therefore let's approach the throne of grace with confidence, so that we may receive mercy and find grace for help at the time of our need. (Hebrews 4:16)

Based on Hebrews 4:16, how are we to approach God? What do we receive when we approach God in this way?

Isn't it comforting to know that we can ask our Creator for assistance when we are in distress? We can freely and without hesitation cry out to Him in our time of need. What does that tell you about the God we serve? God is pleased when we take refuge in Him. *Just breathe in that truth for a moment.*

It was at the Throne of Grace that Habakkuk was reminded of God's sovereignty, power, and faithfulness. God was and is always present. He gives us what we need to take this journey.

> For we walk by faith, not by sight. (2 Corinthians 5:7)

> And without faith it is impossible to please God, for he who comes to God must believe that He is and that He is a rewarder of those who seek Him. (Hebrews 11:6)

Having sincere doubts is different from questioning God's sovereignty. Having an honest question is not wrong. But doubting God without seeking His answers can lead to bitterness and sin. So, when we question God, we must come before Him with the understanding that He loves us and knows what we need better than we do. When we approach God with a humble heart and a teachable mind, we gain a greater understanding of His ways. In the process, He gives us strength and peace for the journey. We learn to accept our frailties and to put our full trust in Him alone.

Let us consider the lessons we can learn from Habakkuk through the lens of other Scripture.

We Can Ask God Honest Questions

> For the eyes of the Lord are on the righteous and His ears are attentive to their prayer, but the face of the Lord is against those who do evil. (1 Peter 3:12)

> And if we know that He hears us, whatever we ask, we know that we have what we asked of Him. (1 John 5:15)

We Must Remain Hopeful

Our faith may be stretched when things take a negative turn in our lives. When we experience disappointment, illness, loss of a job, miscarriage, or a failed marriage, for example, we may struggle with thoughts and emotions that threaten to overwhelm us. These situations make us vulnerable to doubt and unbelief.

Hope deferred makes the heart sick, but desire fulfilled is a tree of life. (Proverbs 13:12)

Why are you cast down, O my soul? And why have you become disturbed within me? Hope in God; for I shall yet praise Him, the help of my countenance and my God. (Psalm 42:11)

Therefore, prepare your minds for action, keep sober in spirit, fix your hope completely on the grace that will be brought to you at the revelation of Jesus Christ. (1 Peter 1:13)

Surely there is a future, and your hope will not be cut off. (Proverbs 23:18)

But if we hope for what we do not see, with perseverance we wait eagerly for it. (Romans 8:25)

And now, Lord, for what do I wait? My hope is in You. (Psalm 39:7)

AS WE PUT OUR COMPLETE HOPE AND TRUST IN GOD, WE GROW IN OUR DEPENDENCE UPON HIM TO DEVELOP A CHRIST-LIKE CHARACTER.

We Must Remain Faithful

There are two distinct viewpoints in life—the secular worldview and the Christian worldview. Those who hold the secular worldview live for the things of this world and are focused on seeking the pleasures of the here and now to please themselves. Those who hold the Christian worldview, however, live to serve the King of kings and the Lord of lords by listening to God, getting direction from Him, and walking faithfully according to His instructions. This results in a life that pleases God. People with a Christian worldview are looking for a better country, *a* heavenly one. They are saved by faith, and between the moment of salvation and the day they die, they choose to walk by faith and not by sight.

> For now, we see in a mirror dimly; but then face to face; now I know in part; but then I shall know fully just as I also have been fully known. (1 Corinthians 13:12)

> Let us hold fast the confession of our hope without wavering, for He who promised is faithful. (Hebrews 10:23)

> For we walk by faith, not by sight. (2 Corinthians 5:7)

We Must Believe God Is Who He Says He Is

Habakkuk was reminded of this when he proclaimed in Habakkuk 3:2, "Lord, I have heard of your fame; I stand in awe of your deeds." We can stand in the gap for the needs of our families, friends, communities, and nation. We answer the call to be God's witnesses by honoring Him as sovereign over all things. We, too, stand in awe of His mighty deeds.

We Must Wait Patiently and Expectantly

God's answers may not come when and how we think they should, but they always come at the right time, and there are lessons to learn as we wait on Him. God promises that His help and His answers will come when we need them most.

> Wait for the Lord; be strong and let your heart take courage; yes, wait for the Lord. (Psalm 27:14)

> Rest in the Lord and wait patiently for Him; do not fret because of him who prospers in his way, because of the man who carries out wicked schemes. (Psalm 37:7)

> Yet those who wait upon the Lord will gain new strength; they will mount up with wings as eagles, they will run and not get tired, they will walk and not become weary. (Isaiah 40:31)

When Habakkuk was frustrated at the beginning of his prophetic book, he came across as being incredibly angry. As he sought God his heart softened. He remembered God's mercy and then prayed "Lord I have heard of your fame; I stand in awe of your deeds, Lord. Repeat them in our day, in our time make them known; in wrath remember mercy." (Habakkuk 3:1).

Instead of letting our *experiences* influence our behavior, we should let our *expectation* of God's power influence our behavior.

We Must Recount His Faithfulness

Remember His faithfulness in the days of old, not just from the Bible, but also in your own life. Think about all the times God has protected and made provision for you and for those you care about.

In the fourth chapter of the Book of Joshua, after God parted the Jordan River so the Israelites could cross onto dry ground, one representative from each of the twelve tribes took a large stone from the middle of the Jordan River and built a monument of twelve stones, one for each tribe.

Joshua then said to the Israelites, "In the future when your children ask you, 'What do these stones mean?' tell them, 'The Lord did this so that all the peoples of the earth might know that the hand of the Lord is powerful and so that you might always fear the Lord your God.'" God told His people to build that monument as a reminder of what God did for the twelve tribes of Israel. We need to remember God's faithfulness when we encounter difficult and challenging situations.

> The Lord God is my strength; He has made my feet like hinds' feet, and makes me walk on my high places. (Habakkuk 3:19)
>
> For the Lord is good; His lovingkindness is everlasting and His faithfulness to all generations. (Psalm 100:5)

REJOICE IN ALL THINGS, AGAIN I SAY REJOICE.

Walk It Out

Habakkuk chose to rejoice even though the circumstances had not changed. He maintained a positive attitude of gratitude. He proclaimed that the Sovereign Lord was his strength.

1. After studying the book of Habakkuk, what can you apply to your own spiritual life?

_____

_____

_____

2. What specific word of encouragement do you want to remember when things get difficult?

_____

_____

_____

3. What questions do you have for God?

_____

_____

_____

4. How did Habakkuk's attitude toward the negative situations change when he gained God's viewpoint?

_____

_____

_____

FROM DOUBT TO CONFIDENCE

Finding Faith in Times of Crisis

In life, you can expect difficulties, tribulations, and trials. Therefore, we must learn how to deal with them. We must practice leaning on God, focusing on His Sovereignty, and looking to Him for understanding. This will teach us how to maintain a positive attitude of hopefulness and gratitude.

Why is this important? It is important because as a follower of His Son, Jesus, God does not want you to live in defeat. And that's exactly where the devil wants you—inactive and ineffective. If you feel defeated, you won't be able to positively impact the world for the kingdom of Christ. *Rise and walk O daughter of the Most High God.*

When challenging times come into your life, ask yourself these questions: What important lessons can I learn from this situation? How can I use this challenge to grow? What choices do I need to make to maintain a godly perspective?

OUR THOUGHTS MATTER. OUR WORDS MATTER. OUR CHOICES MATTER.

Read Deuteronomy 30:19–20

What choice does God want His people to make? How important is this choice?

When you have a Christian worldview, all challenges become learning experiences and growth opportunities. As you increase your reliance on God and seek His strength and wisdom, life's challenges and difficulties will embolden you to step into the battle.

Remember, nothing touches us except what God allows. For reasons unknown to us, God allows such things for our good and His glory. This is what it means to walk by faith.

> Give thanks for everything, for this is God's will for you in Jesus Christ. (1 Thessalonians 5:18)

Learning to protect your internal thoughts will help you to be optimistic rather than pessimistic.

Are you typically optimistic? If so, you tend to see the possibilities and opportunities around you.

Are you typically pessimistic? If so, you tend to see negative outcomes with no hope of positive results.

Matthew Henry, a Bible commentator in the early 18th century, reflected on his view of life when, after being mugged, he said, "Let me be thankful first that I was never robbed before. Although they took my wallet, they did not take my life. It was I who was robbed and not I who robbed."

LEARNING HOW TO MAINTAIN A POSITIVE OUTLOOK ON LIFE IS THE FIRST STEP TO GAINING VICTORY OVER NEGATIVE SITUATIONS.

A pessimist's response to **FEAR** is **F**alse **E**vidence **A**ppearing **R**eal.

Your response to fear is a choice. How often have you given your thoughts and energy to something that *might* happen? How often have you worried about something that never actually happened? It takes energy to manage negativity which is just a phantom barrier in your life. *Phantom* describes something that is *masquerading* as real but is not *actually* real. When phantom barriers are identified they can be dismissed. This frees your thoughts from what might happen to the things that truly need your attention.

> Jesus told us, "The thief comes only to steal and kill and destroy." (John 10:10)

Why is it important to identify *phantom* barriers?

You have an enemy—Satan—who does not want you to succeed. His objective is to wear you down and destroy your faith. He exists to kill, steal, and destroy you and everything you hold dear. If you succumb to this type of thief, then everything that God wants for you will be stolen.

> John 10:10 continues with Jesus saying, "I have come that they may have life and have it to the full."

An optimist's response to **FEAR** is to **F**ace **E**verything **A**nd **R**ise.

When you experience a troubling situation, think about *proactive steps* you can take to diffuse it by using the weapons of God's word and the Full Armor of God.

> And those who know Your name put their trust in You, for You, O Lord have not forsaken those who seek You. (Psalm 9:10)

Read Ephesians 6:10–11

- How do the various pieces of the armor of God help us to stand in the face of fear?
- What practical steps can you take to put on the full armor of God in your daily life?

Read Isaiah 41:10

- What specific reasons does God give for why we should not be afraid?
- How can reflecting on God's strength and presence help you to overcome fear in your life?

Read Hebrews 4:16

- What assurance do we have when approaching God's throne in our time of need?
- How can you apply this verse to your personal prayer life and seek God's help in time of difficulty?

Read Philippians 4:8

- What impact do our thoughts and focus have on our emotions and actions?
- How can you intentionally shift your thoughts to dwell on the things mentioned in this verse in your daily life?

Read Psalm 28:7

- What specific aspects of God did Habakkuk focus on that brought him comfort and strength?
- How can this verse encourage you during times of fear, confusion, and uncertainty in your own life?

  And those who know Your name put their trust in You, for You, O Lord, have not forsaken those who seek You. (Psalm 9:10)

  If any of you lacks wisdom, let him ask God, who gives generously to all without reproach, and it will be given to him. (James 1:5)

Read Deuteronomy 10:12, Psalm 141:3, 2 John 1:8, 1 Timothy 4:16, and James 4:7

How do these verses encourage you in your areas of struggle?

WE MUST SEEK GOD, LISTEN FOR HIS VOICE, AND DO WHAT HE IS CALLING US TO DO.

Therefore let us draw near with confidence to the throne of grace, so that we may receive mercy and find grace to help in time of need. (Hebrews 4:16)

Walk It Out

1. If you succumb to fear, what might you miss out on? How can you change your perspective and approach to avoid missing out on potential opportunities?

_____

_____

_____

2. How can taking an optimistic approach yield a better outcome in your decision-making and problem-solving?

_____

_____

_____

3. In what areas of your life do you need to cast your cares on God and not give in to worry and fear? How can you actively trust God in these areas?

_____

_____

_____

Moving from doubt to confidence:

- Identify and eliminate any phantom barriers in your life that may be holding you back.
- Focus on recognizing obstacles or doubts that prevent your full trust in God's faithfulness and find ways to address these doubts through His promises.
- Find specific Bible passages that remind you of God's faithfulness to boost your confidence and to contemplate what it means to walk by faith.

PERSEVERANCE, FAITH, AND THE BIRTH OF A NATION

Intersection of Faith and Freedom

In 1620, the Pilgrims departed from England to venture into the New World, taking great risks with their lives and future prospects in the pursuit of religious freedom.

As we reflect on the journey of the Pilgrims, we are reminded of their perseverance and determination. They faced countless obstacles on their voyage across the treacherous Atlantic Ocean. With unwavering faith and belief in God's providence, they pressed on.

Upon arrival in the New World, the Pilgrims faced further hardships. Harsh weather conditions, lack of resources, and unfamiliar territory tested their resolve. Yet, they remained steadfast in their commitment to establishing a community where they could freely worship and live according to their beliefs.

The Pilgrims' vision for a society founded on Christian principles set the stage for the birth of our nation. Their journey and sacrifice were not in vain, as their legacy still resonates with us today. The principles of religious freedom, individual liberty, and justice that they held dear formed the bedrock of our nation's founding.

1. How did the Pilgrims demonstrate perseverance and determination throughout their journey?

2. Why were the Pilgrims committed to establishing a community where they could freely worship and live according to their beliefs?

3. How did the Pilgrims' vision for a society founded on Christian principles impact the birth of a new nation?

In 1776, the founding fathers of the United States declared independence from Great Britain. In their pursuit of self-governance, these visionaries acknowledged the fundamental importance of faith and the reliance on Almighty God. They recognized that a strong spiritual foundation was crucial for the establishment of a just and free society.

Consequently, the United States Constitution was built upon the principles of religious freedom, enabling individuals to practice their chosen faith without fear of persecution. This acknowledgment of the role of faith in shaping our nation's values fostered a sense of unity that would prove to be a cornerstone in the formation of the American Constitution and ensured the protection of religious liberty for future generations.

Throughout our history, moments of uncertainty and doubt have tested the resolve of the American people. But, time and time again, we have found strength in our faith and determination. Whether it be the trials endured during the Civil War or the struggles faced during the Civil Rights Movement, the resilience of the American people has shone through. Even in the face of the 9/11 terrorist attacks and subsequent wars abroad, we have remained steadfast, united by a shared faith and an unwavering commitment to the core principles that support this nation.

1. What did the founding fathers recognize as important to build a just and free society?

2. How did the acknowledgment of the role of faith shape the values in the American Constitution?

3. Provide an example from history where the resolve of the American people was tested. How did they overcome it?

4. Why is it important for future generations to be taught this history? Do you think it is necessary to protect religious liberty in America? If so, why or why not?

Today, we find ourselves facing new challenges that test our faith and resolve. Divisions and tensions threaten to erode the very fabric of our society. The values that have guided us for centuries are being challenged and in some cases overthrown. It is up to us to rise to the occasion. We must be the guardians of what those who came before us gave us, ensuring that the flame of freedom is never extinguished.

We must emulate the courage of the Pilgrims and the wisdom of our founders, recognizing that the path forward lies in our commitment to individual liberty and the self-evident truths engraved in our founding documents.

In these uncertain times, we must remember that our strength lies in our faith, in our commitment to each other, and in our unwavering devotion to the principles upon which this nation was built. We need to ask ourselves how we too can step up and be a part of protecting the foundations that the Pilgrims and Founders established.

1. Why is it important for us to be the guardians of what those who came before us gave us?

2. How can we emulate the courage of the Pilgrims and the wisdom of our Founders?

3. Why is it important to remember our faith, our commitment to each other, and our devotion to the principles upon which this nation was built in these uncertain times?

As believers, we have been entrusted with the great commission. We are called to share the gospel and make disciples.

> Go therefore, and make disciples of all nations, baptizing them in the name of the Father and of the Son and of the Holy Spirit, teaching them to observe all that I have commanded you. (Matthew 28:19–20)

We look back at the Pilgrims' courageous journey to the New World, seeking a place where they could freely worship God.

William Bradford gave this reason for their voyage. "We have a great hope and inward zeal of laying some foundation, or at least to make some way thereunto, for the propagating and advancing the gospel of the kingdom of Christ in those remote parts of the world."

In order to protect what the Pilgrims and Founders established we too must remain steadfast in our own pursuit to sustain these liberties. How do we prepare to do this?

We are prepared when we make ourselves ready to represent the self-governing principles found in the Bible that are also reflected in the foundations of our nation. We need to learn the true history of our nation. As we refresh our knowledge of the Constitution we can safeguard the principles and moral values that our country was founded upon. This is the only way that we will be able to defend and uphold these important foundations.

In times of divisiveness, it is crucial for Christians to be salt and light. This means we do not shy away from those who may hold different viewpoints. By listening and sharing our perspectives we can search for common ground and work toward solutions that benefit all. This is where genuine value and respect for others is exemplified.

> You are the salt of the earth; but if the salt has become tasteless, how can it be made salty again? It is no longer good for anything, except to be thrown out and trampled under foot by men. You are the light of the world. A city set on a hill cannot be hidden; nor does anyone light a lamp and put it under a basket, but on the lampstand, and it gives light to all who are in the house. Let your light shine before men in such a way that they may see your good works, and glorify your father who is in heaven. (Matthew 5:13–16)

Our Constitution begins by stating, "We The People." It signifies the undeniable power and resilience of ordinary people who unite as citizens. Therefore, we have a duty to actively engage in elections to help steer the course of our nation's future, ensuring that the choices made today shape our country in the years ahead. Given that our nation's very foundations were shaped by the wisdom of the Bible and aligned with biblical values and principles, it is only natural that believers take up the responsibility to protect and preserve it.

It is vital that we understand the beliefs and values held by judges, mayors, and governors who run for office. We need to know how they align with the true desires of "The People." Our collective Christian voice holds immense influence and must be counted if we are to safeguard and uphold our cherished Judeo-Christian principles. In my county, 78,000 people who profess to be Christians *did not* choose to exercise their right to vote during the last election. Imagine the immense impact if this number were multiplied in every county and city across America. If we want to preserve our nation, we need to let our voices resound loudly and decisively at the ballot box...*for such a time as this.*

Supporting and influencing America's Christian values does not equate to imposing a Christian National Religion. Judeo-Christian principles guided the aspirations of the Pilgrims and Founders. As believers we exercise this same aspiration to guide us as we speak out against injustices, supporting causes that align with our values, and advocate for change. We exercise our rights as believers to uphold our Christian liberties through our Constitution which protects us to freely share and promote the gospel in America.

Real change in society begins in the individual heart and is achieved through morality and its expression in God's people. By living a life of integrity, love, and compassion, we can lead by example and inspire others to embrace these virtues which will help sustain the intention of our faith and of our Constitution.

1. Why is it important to learn the true history of our nation?

2. How can refreshing our knowledge of the Constitution help us safeguard the principles and moral values of our country?

3. How should Christians be salt and light in times of divisiveness?

4. What does the phrase "We The People" signify in the Constitution?

5. Why is it important to understand the beliefs and values of judges, mayors, and governors who are running for office?

6. What impact could voting apathy have among Christians in America?

7. Why is it crucial for your voice to resound loudly and decisively at the ballot box?

Together, we can influence our nation where values, principles, and beliefs are protected and cherished. Let us rise to the occasion and be the change we wish to see.

Be A Light In the Darkness

You can make a difference by being a positive influence and source of encouragement to those around you. Show kindness, love, and compassion toward others. Offer a helping hand whenever possible and spread positivity in your words and actions.

> Let your light shine before men in such a way that they may see your good works, and glorify your Father who is in heaven. (Matthew 5:16)

Be More Like Jesus Each Day

Strive to grow in your faith and become more like Jesus by emulating His character and teachings. Spend time in prayer and meditation, seeking guidance and strength from Him. Reflect on His qualities such as love, forgiveness, patience, and humility, and make an effort to embody them in your daily life.

> But we all, with unveiled face, beholding as in a mirror the glory of the Lord, are being transformed into the same image from glory to glory, just as from the Lord, the Spirit. (2 Corinthians 3:18)

> For you were called to freedom, brethren; only do not turn your freedom into an opportunity for the flesh, but through love serve one another. (Galatians 5:13)

Diligently Study the Bible

The Bible is a valuable resource for deepening your understanding of God's word and strengthening your faith. Set aside regular time for studying the Bible, both by yourself and with others. Actively engage with the text, ask questions, seek understanding, and apply the teachings to your life. This will help you grow spiritually and equip you to make a difference by sharing biblical truths with others.

Be diligent to present yourself approved to God as a workman who does not need to be ashamed, accurately handling the word of truth. 2 Timothy 2:15

Be A Witness for Jesus

Making a difference involves being a living testimony of your faith. Let your actions, words, and attitudes reflect the love and teachings of Jesus. Be intentional about demonstrating Christian values such as honesty, integrity, and forgiveness. Seek opportunities to share your faith when appropriate, whether it's through conversations, acts of service, or simply being a kind and compassionate presence.

> But you will receive power when the Holy Spirit has come upon you; and you shall be My witnesses both in Jerusalem, and in all Judea and Samaria, and even to the remotest part of the earth. (Acts 1:8)

Be A Kingdom Representative

Recognize that you are called to be a representative of God's kingdom on earth. This means acting as an ambassador for Christ and His teachings. Make a difference by being actively involved in your community, showing love and compassion to those in need, and standing up for justice, equality, and truth. Use your unique talents and abilities to contribute positively to the world around you.

> And who knows whether you have not attained royalty for such a time as this? (Esther 4:14)

Walk It Out

Reflect on what aspect of this lesson touched you the most.

Have you felt a connection with a message from God about how you can positively impact the lives of others, whether it be in your immediate circle or in your community?

Remember that simple acts of kindness and faith have the power to trigger a chain reaction and lead to meaningful transformations.

THE CHURCH IN SOCIETY

LESSON 11

The State of America Reflects the State of the Church

This statement holds profound significance in today's society. It serves as a reminder that the well-being and progress of a nation are intricately tied to the condition of its moral compass. The Church serves as a guiding light in society. It has the responsibility to teach and uphold God's principles as responsible citizens are equipped to positively contribute to their family and community.

According to the Bible, God created and instituted three forms of government: the family, the Church, and the civil government. Here are the scriptural references that support the establishment of these three forms of government:

The Family: God established the institution of family as the foundation of society. It consists of a husband, a wife, and their children, and is meant to reflect the relationship between Christ and the Church.

> Then the Lord said, "It is not good for the man to be alone; I will make him a helper suitable for him." (Genesis 2:18)

> God created man in His own image, in the image of God He create him; male and female He created them. God blessed them and said to them, "Be fruitful and multiply, and fill the earth, and subdue it; and rule over the fish of the sea and over the birds of the sky and over every living thing that moves on the earth." (Genesis 1:27–28)

For this reason a man shall leave his father and mother and shall be joined to his wife, and the two shall become one flesh. This mystery is great; but I am speaking with reference to Christ and the Church. (Ephesians 5:31–32)

In the fear of the Lord, there is strong confidence, and his children will have refuge. (Proverbs 14:26)

Parents are given the responsibility for the training and upbringing of their children teaching them in the ways of the Lord, providing discipline and guidance, and setting a positive example for them to follow.

These words, which I am commanding you today, shall be on your heart. You shall teach them diligently to your sons and shall talk of them when you sit in your house and when you walk by the way and when you lie down and when you rise up. (Deuteronomy 6:6–7)

Train up a child in the way he should go, even when he is old, he will not depart from it. (Proverbs 22:6)

The Church: God established the church as a gathering of believers, providing spiritual guidance, instruction, and fellowship. It serves as the body of Christ on earth.

I also say to you that you are Peter, and upon this rock I will build My church; and the gates of Hades will not overpower it. (Matthew 16:18)

And let us consider how to stimulate one another to love and good deeds, not forsaking our own assembling together, as is the habit of some, but encouraging one another; and all the more as you see the day drawing near. (Hebrews 10:24–25)

Civil Government: God instituted civil government to establish order, protect and promote justice, and reward good behavior while punishing evil. The governing authorities are given by God to maintain peace and provide a just society.

Every person is to be in subjection to the governing authorities. For there is no authority except from God, and those which exist are established by God. (Romans 13:1)

For rulers are not a cause of fear for good behavior, but for evil. Do you want to have no fear of authority? Do what is good and you will have praise from the same. (Romans 13:3)

God created and established the family, the Church, and civil government for the well-being and orderliness of human society.

Recent years have tested the Church. We have been pressed on all sides by ever-declining moral standards in our world. The foundations of our Christian republic are under increasing attack.

When the righteous increase, the people rejoice, but when a wicked man rules, people groan. (Proverbs 29:2)

Sadly, the Church has been silent as wickedness has advanced in society. It is only as God's people return to Him, are faithful to Him, and govern themselves according to the Bible that healing can come to our land.

And if My people who are called by My name will humble themselves and pray and seek My face and turn from their wicked ways, then I will hear from heaven, will forgive their sin, and will heal their land. (2 Chronicles 7:14)

The founding fathers believed in the existence of a Creator as the fundamental premise underlying all self-evident truth. They understood that living in accordance with godly intentions provides us with a moral code for conducting our lives. Passivity was never embraced during the early years of America. Religion and piety were seen as essential in promoting the moral fiber of both citizens and government.

It is evident that without religion, the government of a free people cannot be sustained. It is crucial for us to align ourselves with the plumb line of the Bible, to seek God's face and turn from our wicked ways, to ensure that our nation remains blessed by God.

Like the founders of this nation, we must not sit idly by and hope for positive change to happen. We must recognize that our actions and voices are crucial in shaping a better future. If we remain silent in the face of injustice, we allow evil to go unchecked.

It is our duty as followers of Christ to actively engage with the world around us and be intentional disciples to share the hope of the gospel.

> For if you remain silent at this time, relief and deliverance will arise for the Jews from another place, and you and your father's house will perish. And who knows whether you have not attained royalty for such a time as this? (Esther 4:14)

"BLESSED IS THE NATION WHOSE GOD IS THE LORD, THE PEOPLE WHOM HE HAS CHOSEN FOR HIS OWN INHERITANCE." PSALM 33:12

We are called a royal priesthood unto God. We must not conform to the ways of the world but strive to walk in the footsteps of Jesus. By doing so, we become living testimonies of His love and grace.

> But you are a chosen race, a royal priesthood, a holy nation, a people for God's own possession, so that you may proclaim the excellencies of Him who has called you out of darkness into His marvelous light. (1 Peter 2:9)

The work of Christians today extends beyond just attending church and gathering for fellowship. We must BE the Church that is actively engaged with the world around us. This is where the light is to shine – in the darkness. Jesus, Who is full of grace and truth, has given us all we need to live a godly life and to become a true reflection of Him.

At the local level, in the public schools, for example, it is our responsibility to engage when we see decisions made that negatively impact our children's well-being and threaten their innocence.

We must be willing to advocate for truth and righteousness, even when it is unpopular or goes against the prevailing cultural norms. By doing so, we not only protect the values we hold dear but also contribute to the well-being of our community and society as a whole.

The Church was never meant to live in a bubble; rather, we were chosen to go and make disciples of all nations, teaching them to observe the commands that God has given to us.

> Who will stand up for Me against evildoers? Who will take his stand for me against those who do injustice. (Psalm 94:16)

As we represent Jesus in society there will be those who will not want to listen. They may even express anger and rage toward biblical truth. But that should not prevent us from standing up for what is right and good by voicing our values.

We see biblical examples where God's people stood in the gap and did what God called them to do even when it was not popular. People like Nehemiah identified a problem to solve, Esther understood her times, and Noah built an ark without ever seeing rain.

We too have this call to represent Christ in a lost world, but when does this become necessary? When we see evil being called good, and truth being exchanged for a lie. As believers we cannot act in a manner that is contrary to the teachings and requirements of God's word. When truth is blurred and defined as *my truth* or *your truth*, we must give voice and action to protect the truth as defined by God's holy word.

At the core, this is a battle between good and evil, God and satan. The Creator of all things gave us the handbook for truth. We are the voice to stand up and fight for truth to recover those who are blinded by evil.

> With gentleness correcting those who are in opposition, if perhaps God may grand them repentance leading to the knowledge of the truth, and they may come to their senses and escape from the snare of the devil, having been held captive by him to do his will. (2 Timothy 2:25–26)

1. How does the concept of representing Christ in a lost world change in the face of a society that calls evil good and exchanges truth for lies?

2. As believers, how can we avoid acting in a manner that contradicts the teachings and requirements of God's word in a world where truth is often blurred and defined as "my truth" or "your truth"?

3. In the battle between good and evil, God and satan, how can we give voice and take action to protect The Truth as defined by God's word?

4. In what ways can we learn from biblical examples, such as Nehemiah, Esther, Noah, and Paul, about standing in the gap and doing what God calls us to do even in the face of opposition?

5. What does it mean to stand up and fight for truth to recover those who are blinded by evil and how can we do this with gentleness? Give a few examples.

The Church is the sphere of God's government to teach and mobilize the gospel message to all the earth. Active participation connects fellow believers to participate in the outreach to the community using our uniques skills, talents, and giftings. The local church is the place where we should gain fellowship with other believers to strengthen our faith. A healthy church is a place where we as the people of God are equipped for the work of ministry.

> All Scripture is inspired by God and profitable for teaching, for reproof, for correction, for training in righteousness; so that the man of God may be adequate, equpped for every good work. (2 Timothy 3:16–17)

Is your church thriving, fostering trust, effectively discipling members, and fearlessly evangelizing? Does your pastor preach the gospel so that you are learning how to live and impact your home and community for God? Are you learning how to stand in a culture that has lost its compass to effectively respond in your work and in society?

Jesus assigned specific missions and responsibilities to His Church to carry out His plan and for us to be His witnesses in every area of our lives. When a church faithfully teaches the Bible, members are equipped with the knowledge and understanding of how to live together in harmony with others, are guided by God's plumb line, and become shining lights in the community.

The family unit has long been recognized as a source of strength in America, but unfortunately, it is facing immense challenges today. Perverted definitions are being embraced as fact based on personal feelings and opinions. God as our Creator gave the instructions for human beings in the Bible. He provided clear definitions for male and female roles, marriage, parenting, and the first form of government, the family. As our lives are guided by God's plumb line, we can establish a home based on God's design. Remember, a *plumb line* is not a moving target based on individual opinions or preferences; it hangs true no matter what.

A godly home provides children with a moral compass to shape character as they learn about honesty, integrity, compassion, and virtue. This helps to guide their decision-making throughout their lives. This in turn develops good citizens who respect the well-being of others. Sound marriages that thrive are based on commitment, faithfulness, selflessness, and forgiveness. This all has a positive impact on communities because it provides a sense of social responsibility, justice, equality, and compassion.

In a world that often feels chaotic and divisive, the Christian home should be the cornerstone of society, demonstrating security, hope, love, and unity.

> Now may the God of peace Himself sanctify you entirely; and may your spirit and soul and body be preserved complete, without blame at the coming of our Lord Jesus Christ. (1 Thessalonians 5:23)

Seventeenth-Century Dutch Theologian Hugo Grotius Wrote

He knows not how to rule a kingdom, that cannot manage a province; nor can he wield a province that cannot order a city; nor he order a city, that knows not how to regulate a village; nor he a village, that cannot guide a family; nor can that man govern well a family that knows not how to govern himself; neither can any govern himself unless reason be his lord, will and appetite her vassal; nor can reason rule unless herself be ruled by God and wholly obedient to Him."

James B. Rose, A Guide To American Christian Education, 1987
The Christian Principle of Self-Government, 36

Though nearly 400 years old, Grotius's words ring true today.

Statistics show that the rates of divorce, drug addiction, and suicide, are the same Church as in the world. As we realign our hearts to walk in God's ways, over time we can shift the Church's influence in our culture. Once again, a thriving Church will have a positive ripple effect to have a thriving America.

What does the Bible says about marriage and children in the following passages?

Genesis 1:27-28

Hebrews 13:4

Proverbs 18:22

Genesis 2:23-24

Proverbs 22:6

> For if someone does not know how to manage his own household, how will he care for God's Church? (1 Timothy 3:5)

> Look carefully then how you walk, not as unwise but as wise. (Ephesians 5:15)

And God is able to make all grace abound to you, so that having all sufficiency in all things at all times, you may abound in every good work. (2 Corinthians 9:8)

But whoever causes one of these little ones who believe in Me to stumble, it would be better for him to have a heavy millstone hung around his neck, and to be drowned in the depth of the sea. (Matthew 18:6)

If you are a parent, you have been given the immense blessing and sobering responsibility of raising your children in the admonition, or instruction, of the Lord. Teaching them to love God and obey His commandments.

It is not the responsibility of the government, the state, or the school system to raise our children; it is ours alone.

You shall teach them diligently to your children, and shall talk of them when you sit in your house, and when you walk by the way, and when you lie down, and when you rise. (Deuteronomy 6:7)

As parents, it is our duty to impart religious beliefs, ethics, and correct principles to our children. Consequently, children gain appropriate conduct, cultivate good habits, and develop respect toward themselves and others. We need to be vigilant, committed, and thorough when it comes to instructing our children about the truth, ensuring that they are equipped to navigate through a corrupt and immoral society with resilience. Unfortunately, our children and grandchildren are being exposed to things that they should not be exposed to at such an early stage of life. We need to have conversations with them and teach what the Bible says so that when they are exposed to distortions, they have a moral compass in place to discern between what is right and what is wrong. It is imperative that they understand how God created them and know how precious they are in His sight in order to counter the perverted spirit at work in the world.

It is crucial for children to read their Bible so they understand what God is speaking to their heart. God promises to bring light in times of darkness and, through His word, will communicate to this generation.

When gross darkness comes a light will arise:

The people who walk in darkness will see a great light; those who live in a dark land, the light will shine on them. (Isaiah 9:2)

He will speak dreams and visions to the young men:

> It will come about after this that I will pour out My Spirit on all mankind; and your sons and daughters will prophesy, your old men will dream dreams, your young men will see visions. (Joel 2:28)

Parents must be ready to engage in challenging discussions with their children concerning the evil that aims to take away their innocence, cause harm, and ruin their lives. Parents must have the courage to openly communicate the principles and moral standards from a biblical perspective.

> Arise, shine; for your light has come, and the glory of the Lord has risen upon you. (Isaiah 60:1)

Read Matthew 5:13–16, Philippians 2:1–5, 1 Peter 2:12, and Matthew 28:19

How are we to make a positive impact on society?

Read James 1:12

What is the ultimate reward for persevering through hardships?

As Christian women, we have a responsibility to stand firm in our faith and to be a light in the world. Our actions and choices can have a significant impact on our families, communities, and our nation.

The Pilgrims and Founding Fathers laid the foundation for our American Christian heritage, with a vision of religious freedom, liberty, and justice for all. It is up to us to carry on their legacy and to pass it on to future generations.

Walk It Out

1. Do you believe that the Church should tackle societal issues beyond faith? If so, how can it make a positive impact on the community and America?

   _____

   _____

2. How can turning to God and reintegrating the Bible into American life bring healing to marriages, families, and relationships?

   _____

   _____

3. How do your actions create ripples of change in the world, like pebbles in a pond?

   _____

   _____

4. In what ways can a renewed focus on seeking God lead to healing for America?

   _____

   _____

5. How has being a part of a group of believers and deepening your understanding of God strengthened your faith in times of adversity?

   _____

   _____

6. What do you think is your role in God's plan?

   _____

   _____

Look to God to light your way. Trust the words of the prophet Isaiah: "Whether you turn to the right or to the left, your ears will hear a voice behind you saying, 'This is the Way, walk in It.'" (Isaiah 30:21)

RUNNING THE RACE

Finishing Well

As a believer in Jesus Christ, it is important to remember that we are in a race. The Apostle Paul compared the Christian life to an athletic event, urging us to run with patience the race set before us.

In this race, we will face fierce opposition from various sources. The flesh—which represents our old nature, the world—and its current culture; and the devil—who seeks to devour us. However, we must remember that when we align our life in God, we are not alone and can overcome any opposition that comes our way.

> If God is for us, who is against us? He who did not spare His own Son, but delivered Him over for us all, how will He not also with Him freely give us all things? Who will bring a charge against God's elect? (Romans 31:39)

In our present world, there are countless causes, agendas, and lies competing for our attention, all seeking to distract us from following God's will for our lives. In order to overcome this opposition, we need to set our gaze completely on Christ and trust Him to lead us onward.

> For the Lord God helps Me, Therefore, I am not disgraced; Therefore, I have set My face like flint, And I know that I will not be ashamed. (Isaiah 50:7)

This race needs to be run unashamedly with an unwavering commitment to do things God's way. We need to continually pray, **"Not my will, but Thy will be done,"** putting God's desires above our own. By doing this, we can stay focused on the race set before us and run it with endurance, knowing that we will have a heavenly prize waiting at the finish line.

> Do you not know that those who run in a race all run, but only one receives the prize? Run in such a way that you may win. (1 Corinthians 9:24)

Being unashamed in running the race means that we do not shrink back or compromise our beliefs when faced with opposition or pressure to conform. It means that we boldly proclaim the gospel and live out our faith in our daily lives. We must not only talk about our beliefs but we must demonstrate them by the way we love and serve others.

So let us have the courage to stand up for what is right, speak the truth with love, and live lives that reflect the character of Christ. Let us be unashamed witnesses for Jesus, lifting our voices as we disciple others and point people to Jesus as we share the transformative power of His grace.

- Are you prepared to courageously stand up for what is right and make a positive impact in your community?
- Will you wholeheartedly commit to speaking the truth with love and embodying the character of Christ in your daily life?
- Are you ready to fearlessly share the tranformative power of grace and disciple others in their journey of faith?
- What steps are you willing to take to live out your faith unashamedly and inspire others to do the same?
- In what ways can you lift your voice and point people to Jesus within your community and culture?

A Secular Worldview Leads to Eternal Destruction

> Enter through the narrow gate; for the gate is wide and the way is broad that leads to destruction, and there are many who enter through it. (Matthew 7:13)

A Biblical Worldview Leads to Everlasting Life

> Now we have received, not the spirit of the world, but the Spirit who is from God, so that we may know the things freely given to us by God. (1 Corinthians 1:12)

> See to it that there is no one who takes you captive through philosophy and empty deception in accordance with human tradition, in accordance with the elementary principles of the world, rather than in accordance with Christ. (Colossians 2:8)

> For the gate is small and the way is narrow that leads to life, and there are few who find it. (Matthew 7:14)

> But the Spirit explicitly says that in later times some will fall away from the faith, paying attention to deceitful spirits and teachings of demons, by means of the hypocrisy of liars seared in their own conscience as with a branding iron. (I Timothy 4:1–2)

1. In what ways can philosophy and empty deception lead to being taken captive, and how can you guard against this according to God's teachings?

2. What does the small gate and narrow way that leads to live mean for your understanding of the Christian faith, and how do you think this impacts your daily life?

3. According to the warning about falling away from the faith, what are the signs to recognize deceitful spirits and teachings of demons, and how can believers guard against them?

Let us not be deceived by the illusion of safety and comfort. The world may reject our message, but we cannot be discouraged. For it is in the face of opposition that our faith is tested, and our dedication to the Lord is proven. We must be bold and courageous, unafraid to speak the truth and confront the darkness that is trying to infultrate society.

We have been called to be salt and light in this world. It is up to us to preserve the values and principles that are being eroded. We cannot remain silent when lives are being destroyed by violence, perversion, and lies. Do not underestimate the power of your prayers. Seek the Lord with all your heart, and interceed for families, leaders, and our nation. Pray for wisdom and discernment to know how you can best serve your family, friends, and coworkers. Pray for strength and endurance so you keep your eyes on Jesus. Pray for unity among beleivers, that together, we may overcome our differences and stand strong.

The words of Jesus in John 9:4 reminds us of the importance of working while it is still day.

We must carry out the works of Him who sent Me as long as it is day; night is coming, when no one can work. (John 9:4)

The time for laboring in the harvest field is now, for a time will come when the opportunity will be lost.

> Arise and shine; for your light has come, and the glory of the Lord has risen upon you. For behold, darkness will cover the earth, and deep darkness the peoples; but the Lord will rise upon you and His glory will appear upon you. Nations will come to your light, and kings to the brightness of your rising. (Isaiah 60:1-3)

The call is urgent. The time is now. May our hearts burn with the passion to serve God and walk in all of His ways. May we be a church that is awake, alert, and responsive, and may we never forget the promise that awaits those who stay on the narrow path, for in so doing, we will see others come to know the love and salvation of Jesus Christ. Let us not shrink back, but let us press on and fight the good fight.

As I Fight The Fight Of Faith I Am Committed To

- Answer the urgent call to make a difference now.
- Be filled with passion to serve God and walk in His ways.

- Remain wide-awake and be part of a responsive church that is eager to fulfill God's purpose in society.
- Stay on the narrow path and witness to others to know, love, and embrace the salvation that comes through Jesus Christ.
- Stand strong in the face of challenges, refusing to shrink back, and instead, press on with courage and faith, knowing the victory is ours in Christ.

Put on the full armor of God, so that you will be able to stand firm against the schemes of the devil. For our struggle is not against flesh and blood, but against the rulers, against the powers, against the world forces of this darkness, against the spiritual forces of wickedness in the heavenly places. Therefore, take up the full armor of God, so that you will be able to resist in the evil day, and having done everything, to stand firm. Stand firm therefore, having girded your loins with truth, and having put on the breastplate of righteousness, and having shod your feet with the preparation of the gospel of peace; in addition to all, taking up the shield of faith with which you will be able to extinguish all the flaming arrows of the evil one. And take the helmet of salvation, and the sword of the Spirit, which is the word of God. With all prayer and petition pray at all times in the Spirit, and with this in view, be on the alert with all perseverance and petition for all the saints. (Ephesians 6:10–18)

In the midst of a world filled with challenges and distractions, it is crucial that we as sisters in Christ remain steadfast and focused on God's truth. The Author and finisher of our faith is Jesus Christ, and it is through Him that we find the strength and guidance to navigate through life's obstacles.

We must persevere and refuse to give up, knowing that God is able to keep us from stumbling. In times of plagues, natural disasters, financial turmoil, and distressing world events, our eyes should be fixed on Jesus, who will lead us through. Even as we witness the moral decline in our society, it is essential that we keep our focus on Him and not be swayed by the darkness around us.

As members of the Church, we are called to stand together, pray together, and support one another. By keeping our eyes on Jesus, we can stand firm against the schemes of the devil and the spiritual forces of wickedness. Let us put on the full armor of God, equipping ourselves with truth and righteousness, the gospel of peace, faith, salvation, and the word of God.

Be strong in the Lord and rely on His strength as you run the race set before you. Persevere with all prayer and petition, remaining alert and persistent in prayer. Remember that your ultimate goal is to stand in the presence of His glory, blameless and with great joy.

As you press on in faith, give all glory, majesty, dominion, and authority to God your Savior, through Jesus Christ your Lord. Trust that He will guide you and prepare you for the day when He returns for His Bride, the Church.

> Now to Him who is able to keep you from stumbling, and to make you stand in the presence of His glory, blameless with great joy, to the only God our Savior, through Jesus Christ our Lord, be glory, majesty, dominion, and authority, before all time and now and forever. AMEN! (Jude 24–25)

> Finally, be strong in the Lord and in the strength of His might. Put on the full armor of God, so that you will be able to stand firm against the schemes of the devil. (Ephesians 6:10–11)

> His master replied, Well done good and faithful servant! You have been faithful with a few things; I will put you in charge of many things, enter into the joy of your master." (Matthew 25:23)

As you navigate the journey set before you, it is important to remember that you are in a spiritual battle. Battles require a strategy and battle plan to overcome the enemy, especially when faced with strong opposition. So, how can you stay encouraged and motivated in the face of adversity?

A Battle Plan To Help Guide You

1. **Cultivate the right beliefs to live the way God intended:** Seek God's truth through His word and align your beliefs with His principles. Let His truth guide your thoughts and actions.
2. **Understand your value and walk out your unique purpose:** Recognize that you are fearfully and wonderfully made by God. Discover your gifts, talents, and passions, and use them to fulfill the purpose God has for your life.

3. **Live proactively, not reactively:** Rather than simply reacting to circumstances, take initiative. Be intentional in seeking God's will and actively pursuing His plans for your life.

4. **Develop a strong root system to produce godly fruits:** Deepen your relationship with God through prayer, worship, and study of His word. Allow His truth to anchor you and bear the fruit of love, joy, peace, patience, kindness, goodness, faithfulness, gentleness, and self-control.

5. **Determine to fight the good fight and finish the race well:** Stay committed to following Jesus, even when faced with challenges. Persevere in your faith, staying strong and focused on the ultimate prize of eternal life with Him.

6. **Shine the light of truth to make a difference in this world:** Share the gospel and let your life be a testimony of God's love and grace. Live with integrity, compassion, and humility, impacting those around you with the light of God's truth.

You Are Not Alone in This Battle

Call upon the Holy Spirit for guidance, strength, and encouragement. Trust in God's promises, knowing that He is with you every step of the way. Stay faithful, pressing on toward the goal, eagerly desiring to hear those cherished words from Jesus: "Well done, good and faithful servant."

> How blessed are those whose ways are blameless, who walk according to the law of the Lord. How blessed are those who observe His testimonies, who seek Him with all their heart. They do no unrighteousness. They walk in His ways. You have ordained Your precepts, that we should keep them diligently. Oh, that my ways may be established to keep Your statutes! Then I shall not be ashamed when I look upon all Your commandments. I shall give thanks to You with an upright heart when I learn Your righteous laws. I shall keep Your statues; do not forsake me utterly! How can a young man keep his way pure? By keeping it according to Your word. With all my heart I have sought You; do not let me wander from your commandments. Your word I have treasured in my heart, that I may not sin against You. Blessed are You, O Lord; teach me Your statutes. (Psalm 119: 1–12)

> I have fought the good fight, I have finished the course, I have kept the faith; in the future there is laid up for me the crown of

righteousness, which the Lord, the righteous Judge, will award to me on that day; and not only to me, but also to all who have loved His appearing. (2 Timothy 4:7–8)

You will seek Me and find Me when you seek Me with all of your heart. (Jeremiah 29:13)

1. How can you rely on the Holy Spirit for guidance, strength, and encouarement as you prepare for the race?

2. In what ways can you trust in Gods promises and remember that He is with you every step of the way during the race?

3. What does it mean to observe His testomonies and seek Him with all your heart? How can you incorportate this into your training and mindset for the race?

Read Colossians 1:16–17

As you focus on the race set before you, how can this verse provide you with the necessary strength to endure and persevere?

The Goal Is Simple

The goal is to align our lives with the plumb line of God's word and exhibit godly values and character in everything we do. Through this, we can make a lasting impact in our homes, workplaces, churches, schools, and communities.

To understand where you can make the most meaningful impact, look at the Seven Mountains of Societal Influence. These mountains include the areas of religion, family, education, government, media, arts & entertainment, and business. Identify the area where your influence can make the greatest difference.

Of the Seven Mountains of Societal Influence where do you believe your impact will be most noteworthy?

Consider first your family, where you have the opportunity to instill godly values and lead by example. Alternatively, your impact may be felt most significantly in your workplace or church, where you can positively influence those around you. Focus your efforts on where you can most effectively make a transformative impact. As you embrace this challenge, commit yourself to finishing the race well.

Trust in God's power and guidance as you live a life that brings glory to His name. Together, one life at a time, shining His light in our spheres of influence we can make a difference and help to restore America's godly heritage.

> Therefore go and make disciples of all nations, baptizing them and teaching them to observe all that I have commanded you. (Matthew 28:19)

> Do you not know that those who run in a race all run, but only one receives the prize? Run in such a way that you may win. (1 Corinthians 9:24)

> The righteous person will flourish like the palm tree, she will grow like a cedar in Lebanon. Planted in the house of the Lord, she will flourish in the courtyards of our God. She will still yield fruit in advanced age; She will be full of sap and very green, to declare that the Lord is just; He is my rock, and there is no malice in Him. (Psalm 92: 12–15)

Throughout this study, we have explored the depths and richness of biblical principles that can bring about transformation in our lives. However, it is not enough to just acquire knowledge and understanding of these principles. We must take intentional steps to apply them daily in our life.

As you continue on your journey, I encourage you to regularly revisit these truths. Remind yourself of the wisdom they hold and seek ways to integrate them into your thoughts, words, and actions. Allow them to become ingrained within you, just as breathing comes naturally. Above all, prioritize the discipline of immersing yourself in God's word each day. This spiritual nourishment is crucial for a vibrant Christian life. Through consistent time spent in God's presence, you gain the mind of Christ and will be equipped to respond to the challenges that life presents as well as meet the needs of those around you. Indeed, God has placed you here for a purpose, and His word provides the guidance and strength you need to fulfill it.

It is important to remember that you are not alone on this journey. Together, let us inspire, influence, and impact other like-minded women who share the same desire to make a lasting difference by knowing Jesus Christ and making Him known. By uniting our efforts and encouraging one another, we can work toward reversing the downward trajectory of our nation.

So, as you go forward from this study, may you commit to applying these principles in your life, nurturing your relationship with God through His word, and join hands with fellow believers to bring about positive change. You have been given the tools and the power through Christ to make a significant impact. Together, we can make a lasting impact and shine as a beacon of hope and light in this world.

BE A LIGHT
IT'S SIMPLY TIME

Inspire. Influence. Impact.

CHRISTIAN WOMEN SHINING *THE LIGHT OF CHRIST* IN THE DARKNESS

Printed in the United States
by Baker & Taylor Publisher Services